THE RENEWABLE WAY

Straight talk about restoring our climate, preventing untold suffering, and making a better world.

James Leach

STA Publishing

Published November 2024

Revised September 2025

ISBN: 979-8-218-55738-6

CONTENTS

PREFACE

Our continued use of fossil fuels is unsustainable, not because we will run out, but because doing so will make our planet uninhabitable.

– James Leach, *The Sustainable Way*

This booklet is a follow-up to my 2016 booklet *The Sustainable Way– Straight talk about global warming–what causes it, who denies it, and the common-sense transition to renewable energy.* The public's perception about the consequences of our warming world have changed in the ensuing years. With the obvious examples of rising sea level and increasing extreme weather bringing more destructive winds and flooding, scorching heat, withering drought, and devastating wildfires, the focus has shifted to taking action to mitigate and adapt to our changing world. Central to avoiding the approaching climate crisis is the elimination of the emissions from the burning of fossil fuels, such as coal, oil, and natural gas, formed from the ancient carbon and hydrogen remains of livings organisms [1].

Renewable energy is a political "hot potato," not only because it will shift the balance of wealth and power away from those who provide coal, oil, and natural gas, it will also require all of us to replace the fossil fueled equipment we use to generate electricity, produce heat, and power industries and transportation. The greatest fortunes on Earth are based on fossil fuels. Those who possess this incredible wealth are showing few signs of willingly supporting the transition to renewable energy. They continue to put forth outright lies and disinformation that is delaying and discouraging organized efforts to transition to renewable energy.

Fortunately, emission-free renewable energy is proving to be far less costly than fossil fuels. Though the transition to renewables is inevitable, considerable resistance remains, not only from fossil fuel interests, but also among the general public. Overcoming this requires an awareness of the financial savings and the many other advantages of using renewable energy, and how the transition can be accomplished in an equitable and orderly fashion.

There are many good sources of information about renewable energy and how we can make the transition. The problem is that much of it is not very approachable. My purpose is to provide a plainspoken source that will inspire and guide people through the renewable energy transition. This booklet moves at a rapid pace and is best absorbed when you are in a place where you can take it all in. This material will be of interest to anyone concerned about the climate crisis. And if you, or someone you know, is likely to read only one book on this subject, this is the book!

INTRODUCTION

Renewable energy is energy derived from natural sources that are replenished at a higher rate than they are consumed. – United Nations

Our world is awash in renewable energy. Utilizing it to replace fossil fuels will require us to power everything with electricity generated using this endless energy source. We already have the technology to accomplish this using electricity generated from solar, wind, moving water, and the Earth's heat. This will require less land area than the fossil fuel industry it is replacing and result in far less environmental harm. The lower overall costs to harness this energy, that literally falls freely upon us, is a major factor favoring the transition. Not only will we save in what energy costs us directly, we will also eliminate the staggering costs that our use of fossil fuels imposes on society. Research has shown that today's global economy would be nearly 20% larger, about $20 trillion more, without the accumulated global warming emissions that have already occurred [2]. The societal costs from air pollution and other environmental damage from our use of fossil fuels further burdens the global economy by $ trillions more every year.

The harm from our use of fossil fuels is not equally distributed. As our climate continues to warm and becomes more destabilized, regions that are already hot will experience more unproductive and unlivable conditions. Those living near ocean shores will directly face sea level rise. Some regions will have reduced rain, others more, and weather events everywhere will be far more extreme. Poorer nations will be less capable of adapting to the changing conditions. The wealthy fossil fuel using nations of the northern hemisphere disproportionally burden everyone else with their pollution and greenhouse gas emissions.

Although it may take decades to build out the United States energy infrastructure for this transition, it faces no un-surmountable material or physical barriers. It is going to take some time to educate the public, unwind the established fossil fuel industry stranglehold on our politics, ramp up the production and storage of renewable energy, and replace our fossil fuel powered equipment. Research shows that a fully renewable energy powered world is achievable well before 2050 [1].

Who should lead the way? The United States is responsible for 25% of the increase of greenhouse gases that have accumulated in the atmosphere since the beginning of the industrial age–far more than any other nation [3]. In 2022, United States annual emissions of the primary greenhouse gas carbon dioxide was 32,965 pounds per person (15 metric tons), compared to China at 17,618 pounds per person (8 metric tons) [4]. China invested $546 billion in clean energy in 2022 compared to the United States investment of only $141 billion [5]. In 2022 the United

States emitted far more carbon dioxide per person than China, and invested much less to transition to renewable energy.

China surpassed the United States as the largest emitter of carbon dioxide in 2006. This was largely because so many major nations had outsourced much of their production of goods to China [6]. Studies have estimated that if the greenhouse gas emissions embodied in the products we import were included in United States' emissions, our consumption-based emissions would be as much as 35% [7] higher than the emissions that occur only within our territory. A consumption-based accounting would also significantly reduce China's emissions. We should not feel good about having reduced the emissions that occur within our borders, only because much of the products we consume are now produced elsewhere. As we consume products, we are responsible for the emissions making and shipping them produce.

The United States economy is the envy of the world. With only 4% of global population (333 million / 8 billion), our economy (i.e., Gross Domestic Product) represents more than 25% of the global economy (2023: U.S. = $27 trillion, Global = $105 trillion) [8]. Our average per-person economic value is more than 8 times that of the rest of the world. Those who are the most responsible for the global suffering from fossil fuel emissions, and who have and continue to benefit the most at the expense of the rest of the world, should take the lead. If we do not, who will?

We stand to benefit tremendously from the transition to renewable energy. Not only will we significantly lower our energy costs, we will also have a much more stable and abundant energy supply. The public health and environmental benefits from eliminating the harmful pollution from fossil fuels are beyond measure. And the build-out and ongoing support of renewable energy will invigorate our economy. It will also put an end to the staggering level of government subsidies gifted to the fossil fuel industry and their corrupting political influence. With abundant perpetual energy independence, we will no longer feel the economic pain from global fossil fuel supply manipulation by fossil fuel cartels. And by taking the lead on cutting fossil fuel use, we will begin to defund hostile fossil fuel revenue-dependent nations like Russia and Iran, and turn their focus toward peaceful cooperation and trade rather than the use of military force and terrorism to settle territorial and ideological goals, or to satisfy the whims of their autocratic leaders.

1 - MISERY AND DEGRADATION

Suffering is necessary until you realize it is unnecessary. – Eckhart Tolle, philosopher, and author

On our present course of continuing to burn ever more fossil fuels, all humankind is facing truly hellish conditions. As we consider why we must transition to renewable energy, it is important to understand the misery and degradation from our use of fossil fuels we are seeking to avoid.

Hot, Hungry, Dumb, and Sick

+ 1.8⁰ Fahrenheit and Rising Fast

The Earth's average global temperature has increased by more than 1.8^0 Fahrenheit (1^0 Celsius) since preindustrial times in 1750. This is primarily due to the accumulated atmospheric emissions produced when fossil fuels are burned [9]. This increase in temperature has significantly destabilized our climate, with much more heat energy and water in our atmosphere, causing our warmer oceans to rise as they expand and frozen water on land is melting. We are increasingly experiencing more extreme weather with severe droughts, wildfires, intense rainstorms, and destructive winds. On our present course, with expected growth in our use of fossil fuels, the Earth's average temperature will increase another $.9^0$ F ($.5^0$ C) before midcentury, bringing the temperature increase since pre-industrial times to nearly 3^0 F (1.7^0 C). This will further intensify weather extremes and sea level rise, making many regions around the world unproductive and uninhabitable. Continuing with business-as-usual through the end of the century, Earth's average temperature will increase by as much as 7^0 F (4^0 C) over preindustrial times. This will result in calamitous conditions across the globe.

When we hear of global warming causing an increase in global average temperature of a few degrees Celsius, it does not seem like much of an increase to most people. Many Americans are not familiar with Celsius temperatures. Each degree of Celsius temperature change is equal to 1.8 degrees Fahrenheit change. More importantly, the average global temperature increase does not describe the temperature most people will experience where they live. Seventy percent of the Earth's surface is ocean where water evaporation carries heat into the atmosphere and there is little concentration of heat near the surface as water circulates and there are no hard surfaces that hold heat. The situation is different for land areas, especially those far inland with rock, concrete, asphalt, and other materials that absorb and hold heat. Cities and regions that already have a hot climate will see increases that far exceed the global average increase. And because the Polar regions are warming more than the global average, the customary upper-level atmospheric steering currents are shifting, causing more pronounced and prolonged extreme temperatures to settle over large regions. As our world continues to warm, millions more people will be exposed to life threatening heat. High temperatures also contribute to increased infant mortality and poor infant health. We will all suffer from increasing temperatures. Many will die.

Reduced Nutrition

Elevated atmospheric carbon dioxide is known to stimulate plant growth. Although this sounds like a good thing, it has the unfortunate effect of increasing the proportion of carbohydrate content in plants while reducing the level of proteins and essential minerals [10]. With our current elevated level of atmospheric carbon dioxide, food crops such as wheat, soybean, corn, and rice already have proportionally more carbohydrates than if they were grown in the past. As our carbon dioxide concentration continues to increase, this imbalance will grow. Public health problems related to excess carbohydrate consumption and nutritional deficiencies will likely worsen.

With oceans warming and now 30% more acidic from the increase of carbon dioxide dissolved in the water, the web of ocean life is changing in ways that threatens the food supply of billions of people around the world who rely on the sea. It reduces the carbonate (CO_3) available to shell creatures that form much of the ocean food chain. High ocean acidity and temperatures also cause coral bleaching. This is especially alarming as coral reefs are the home and breeding grounds for countless forms of sea life. Because warmer water holds less dissolved oxygen, all aquatic animals will suffer in a warming world. Our oceans are also facing oxygen depleted dead zones from algae blooms fed by the combination of elevated carbon dioxide, high temperatures and excess fertilizer runoff. As the algae dies, the microbes that digest it consume all the dissolved oxygen in the water, suffocating marine life.

Excess heat, drought, increased environmental acidification, climate shifts, rising seas, and stronger storms all contribute to reduced crop production. These conditions also favor a variety of food crop diseases and pests. Excessive heat has already significantly reduced the numbers of some of our most important pollinators. Elevated levels of atmospheric carbon dioxide also cause plants that compete with food crops to grow more quickly. Freshwater lakes, their tributaries, and coastal estuaries are experiencing die-offs from high water temperatures and algae blooms.

Food insecurity is already a serious problem in many parts of the world. We are looking at a future when food production in many more regions will cease or be much less productive.

On our business-as-usual path of continuing the use of fossil fuels, having sufficient food and a properly balanced diet will be increasingly more difficult. Many will suffer from hunger and malnutrition, and die from starvation.

Reduced Intellectual Performance

Poor nutrition and hunger interfere with all aspects of cognitive performance. Exposure to high temperatures interferes with our ability to concentrate, to learn, and to make good decisions. It also makes it harder to have restful sleep, further hampering our mental performance. As our world becomes hotter, more people are being exposed to mind-numbing heat. In the developed world, people are increasingly retreating to air-conditioned spaces to avoid the heat. But in outdoor and un-air-conditioned spaces, there is no escape.

Acid rain–formed from sulfur dioxide, nitrogen dioxide, and carbon dioxide emissions from burning fossil fuels–has increased the acidification of our land and water. One of the many consequences of this is increasing levels of harmful metals released from soil and materials containing them [11]. Lead is especially toxic as exposure to it contributes to learning disabilities and lower IQ.

Exposure to black carbon soot, various metals, nitrogen dioxide and other forms of fossil fuel combustion air pollution have been associated with developmental disorders, dementia, and reduced cognitive performance. Fine and ultrafine air pollution particulates enter the brain through the olfactory nerve in the upper part of the nose. Cognitive function is also hampered by reduced oxygen supply to the brain from respiratory and cardiovascular diseases caused by fossil fuel air pollution. Our exposure to fossil fuel air pollution shrinks our collective intelligence.

Breathing elevated levels of carbon dioxide reduces our ability to pay attention. If you have ever experienced feeling drowsy in a crowded room, you have likely experienced this. In a confined space where there are sources of carbon dioxide–like humans breathing or poorly vented combustion sources–the accumulation of carbon dioxide can quickly reach levels where our thinking is impaired. It clouds our judgment, hinders complex problem solving, and diminishes learning [12] [13] [14].

During the Covid-19 Pandemic, inexpensive carbon dioxide monitors became popular because they are a good indicator of how well indoor occupied spaces are ventilated. Their widespread use has highlighted the fact that the level of carbon dioxide in classrooms, meeting rooms, offices, and our homes commonly reaches over 1,000 parts per million. Such exposure is above the threshold of cognitive impairment. You should avoid studying, taking exams, driving, or making important life decisions when breathing such high levels of carbon dioxide. It also interferes with sleep quality, which further hampers cognitive performance. With adequate ventilation, the carbon dioxide level will come down to the outdoor background level. This can be difficult when spaces do not have heat recovery ventilation systems because people are sometimes reluctant to open windows.

The level of atmospheric carbon dioxide has just recently passed 420 parts per million (i.e., .042% of the atmosphere), a level that is 50% higher than the 280 parts per million at the start of the industrial revolution in 1750 when large scale burning of fossil fuels began. With this increase in the background level, it is now harder to keep the carbon dioxide level of indoor spaces at a healthy level. On our present course, as we continue burning fossil fuels, the background level of carbon dioxide will likely rise to about 550 parts per million at midcentury, and on up beyond 750 parts per million by 2100. We are facing a time in the not-so-distant future when everyone breathing untreated air will be cognitively impaired. Not only is burning fossil fuels dumb, it is making us dumber!

Allergies, Disease, and Mental Stress

A warmer world favors the spread of many infectious diseases. Bacterial and viral diseases spread by insects such as mosquitoes, ticks, and fleas will have a wider range and longer season in a warmer climate. Warmer conditions also favor viral illnesses spread by mammals such as hantavirus and rabies. Food and water borne illnesses caused by parasites such as crypto and giardia, and bacteria such as Salmonella also favor warmer conditions. Bacteria such as anthrax and the fungi that cause valley fever and histoplasmosis are bolstered in hotter conditions. Marine algal bloom-associated illness also will be more common as will vibriosis–an infection caused by bacteria found in marine environments (Center for Disease Control).

As research into super-spreader events during the Covid Pandemic has shown, elevated carbon dioxide levels increase the transmission rate of respiratory viruses by creating a more favorable alkalinity level in the droplets that transport these viruses through the air [15]. Warmer conditions are already causing longer and more severe allergy seasons. With mental health stressors from climate change multiplying, maintaining one's mental health will become an ever more challenging concern. Human suffering will increase greatly in a hotter world. [16].

Fossil Fuel Pollution

We have long lived with the insidious lethality of air pollution from our use of fossil fuels. It ever so slowly damages our cardiovascular and respiratory systems, and causes or contributes to developmental disorders, various types of cancer, asthma, type-2 diabetes, dementia, and vision loss. This pollution, that slowly penetrates deep into our lungs, bloodstream, and throughout our bodies, is often hard to notice. Most people do not give air pollution a moment's notice, except when they see or smell it. Here is one of countless example to consider. The next time you smell gasoline, you are breathing many harmful vapors, including benzene, a hydrocarbon that always interferes with cell function and causes blood disorders, such as leukemia.

One reason that many people are not keenly aware of the risk from air pollution is because it has been downplayed in our public discourse. Although medical professionals know that air pollution is harmful, our treatment-oriented healthcare system does little to warn us of the long-term risk or of how to prevent harm from it. The slow accumulation of damage from air pollution prevents us from being aware of the danger, leaving many who fall ill to conclude that their suffering has an unavoidable natural cause.

Government reporting of air quality is not always proactive. When air pollution is obvious, either by smell or sight, action may follow if enough influential people take notice. But when it comes to hard to notice pollution, not so much. Reporting tends toward providing enough information to warn of short-term hazards, but not enough to provoke anxiety about long-term exposure.

The United States Environmental Protection Agency (EPA) has a reporting system for a variety of air pollutants. Each is reported separately with ratings at six levels with the lowest risk level colored green and titled "GOOD." This Air Quality Index (AQI) rating is logically interpreted by most people to mean that it is safe; however, in the EPA's words "The AQI focuses on health effects that may be experienced within a few hours or days after breathing polluted air" [17]. It does not describe effects that may be experienced over long periods.

The EPA "GOOD" range for PM2.5, meaning particulate matter measuring 2.5 micrometers or less, spans up to a weight of 12 micrograms per cubic meter (i.e., a cube measuring 39 inches on each side). These are very tiny particles, ranging in size up to about the diameter of a red blood cell and down to those so small they are only visible through an electron microscope. The World Health Organization (WHO) guidelines state that annual average concentrations of PM2.5 should not exceed five micrograms per cubic meter, while 24-hour average exposures should not exceed 15 micrograms per cubic meter more than three to four days per year [18]. Most urban regions and many rural areas in the United States exceed this level. For example, the San Francisco Bay Region's annual average air quality index for PM2.5 is about eight micrograms per cubic meter [19] and with many days annually in and above the MODERATE level of the scale. Breathing this EPA-rated "GOOD" level of PM2.5 most of the time may not produce noticeable harm in the short term, but living in it, decade upon decade, will definitely have negative health consequences that most people will not associate with their long-term exposure.

Another example of harmful pollution is ground-level ozone, which is a gas linked to fossil-fuel emissions that always does serious damage as we breath it. When ozone contacts organic tissue, such as on plants or in our lungs, it burns (i.e., oxidizes) the tissue. The accumulated microscopic scaring of our bronchial passages and lungs contributes to diseases such as bronchitis, chronic obstructive pulmonary disease (COPD), and emphysema. Ground-level ozone is present wherever smog forms. Cities and regions across the United States experience high ozone levels on hot sunny days. Ozone formation will worsen as temperatures rise and more smog forms.

Other fossil-fuel combustion emissions such as carbon soot, sulfur dioxide, nitrogen dioxide, various hydrocarbons, metal particles, and organic aerosols linked to fossil fuels are also very harmful. More than one in ten Americans suffer from chronic lung disease [20]. According to the World Health Organization, 99% of the global population breaths air that contains high levels of pollution resulting in 7 million global premature deaths annually [21]. It is important to recognize that just counting the premature deaths does not begin to express the suffering and cost air pollution causes.

We do not have to live with this! We now have zero emission choices to eliminate our exposure to all of the harmful particulates, and the other pollutants from burning fossil fuels. The public health benefits from eliminating this exposure are truly enormous. It comes down to a simple choice: Do we want to prevent the serious harm it causes to all of us or don't we?

Environmental Destruction

Intense Storms

The atmosphere holds about 7% more water vapor for every 1.8^0 F (1^0 C) increase in temperature [22]. Heat released as water condenses in the atmosphere is what drives storm formation. When storms form in our warmer and wetter atmosphere, they release more heat energy, increasing their updraft and drawing in yet more air and water vapor, further intensifying their strength. The entire natural world is already suffering from far more frequent and catastrophic storms. The intensity of storms will continue to increase as our climate warms.

Drier and Hotter

Rising temperatures will cause drought prone regions to experience even greater loss of water and more intense drought. Water shortages, crop failures, and wildfires will follow, at least while there is still something left to burn. The landscapes of vast regions of the world are changing. For example, much of the west slope of the California Sierra Nevada Mountains is expected to transition from forest to desert-like scrub in just the next few decades [23]. Forests across the northern hemisphere are dying because the warmer climate is allowing pests, like bark beetles, to thrive through the winter. Life will be different for the flora and fauna we now so value. There will be much lost.

Habitat Loss

In many locations natural adaptation will not keep up with the rate of climate change. Over thousands of years, as temperatures and water conditions fluctuate, plants and animals can slowly move as their favored habitat shifts. But with the rapid climate changes we are now experiencing, adapting will not be possible for many species. Plants that need to move to stay within a livable habitat will not always be capable of making the move because the rate they can move is limited by how easily their seeds travel and their rate of growth. And for life-forms restricted by elevation or other barriers, they will not be able to move. Many animals are already finding that as they arrive in their migratory habitats, the conditions and food they depend on are not there. Even those that do not migrate are threatened as environmental changes from pollution and climate change interfere with established food sources essential to their lifecycle. The animals, insects, plants, and microscopic life-forms that collectively make up the natural world are all suffering from these changes. Birds are a good indicator of just how damaging climate change has already become. The National Audubon Society warns that climate change endangers two-thirds of all North American birds. Our warming climate is harming every level of the natural world.

Rising Seas

The warming of oceans and melting of land-based ice and snow is causing our seas to rise. Globally, several billion people are facing the trauma of dislocation this century as they retreat from the shore. This also means that much of the food production, fresh water supplies, and infrastructure in coastal areas will be impacted. On our current course with high global greenhouse emissions, the United States is expected to experience average sea level rise of 7 feet by 2100 and 13 feet by 2150 [24]. Due to differences in uplift and subsidence (i.e. sinking) of land, and differences in water temperature, the amount of sea level rise will vary. For example, along the Gulf Coast, the sea will rise more because of subsidence in the region and because the hotter ocean waters there will expand more.

In most instances, building barriers will not provide lasting protection as the rising waters wear away the barriers, increase shoreline erosion, and seep into the land. In many places where hazardous materials have been carelessly buried, the rising water table will carry it into the open environment causing yet more harm. The entire United States East Coast, Gulf Coast, and large portions of the West Coast, like San Francisco Bay and Puget Sound, will suffer from significant seawater intrusion.

Loss of Permafrost Soil

Another closely related result from the loss of snow- and ice-covered land is the melting of permafrost soils. As methane trapped in the ice crystals escapes into the atmosphere, it adds to the already high level of this powerful greenhouse gas. Considerable harm will also come from other contents released from water crystals or flushed from the soil from the melting water. Many rivers in the far north are running with off-colored water because of metals released from increased ice melt. Trapped carbon dioxide is also being released as well as organic matter that will decompose to produce more carbon dioxide and methane. Dried peat deposits and boreal forests will also increase the incidence of wildfires. The other major harm from permafrost melting is the physical collapse of infrastructure that is no longer supported by firm frozen ground.

Shifting Ocean Currents

Our oceans are home to powerful currents that circulate water and transfer heat from one region to another. These are driven by a combination of prevailing winds and turnover in the water as dense saline water flows to the ocean floor. The formation of sea ice is a primary source for dense saline water as salt is forced out of water when surface sea ice forms. As the polar seas and atmosphere warm, less sea ice is forming resulting in a weakening of the associated ocean currents. A related factor is the increased melting of land-based ice from a warmer atmosphere. This fresh water entering the polar oceans is diluting the salinity, further weakening the currents. The combined effect is to destabilize the climate of those regions where these currents have historically cooled the seas, as well as those regions that receive heat from the currents. And because the currents carry nutrients that sustain much ocean life, this also destabilizes the natural world in these regions.

As just one example, significant weakening of the Atlantic Gulf Stream will have devastating consequences for the British Isles and Scandinavia by reducing the moderating heat it now transports to the region. It will also increase the heat and sea rise along North America's East Coast. Delaying action to stop global warming will only make the situation worse, and perhaps push past a tipping point where stabilization or some recovery of ocean currents on a human timescale may be impossible.

Shifting Atmospheric Currents

The temperature difference between polar and equatorial regions contribute to the stability and strength of the upper-level steering currents that influence how areas of high and low pressure move across the globe. As our planet has warmed, the northern polar region's loss of reflective ice and snow cover has caused it to warm much more than the global average. The resulting reduction in temperature difference between the arctic and equatorial regions has caused the weakened upper-level steering currents of the northern hemisphere to meander from their customary wavy west to east pattern and sometimes to hold weather systems in place for prolonged periods. This has resulted in both longer and more intense heat waves and cold spells, often at latitudes unaccustomed to these extremes. This has caused havoc as the infrastructure is not designed for such extremes, nor are the people and wildlife accustomed to dealing with it. These events will become more severe as our world continues to warm.

Insecurity

Climate-Driven Migration

Climate changes are making many regions of the world unproductive or unlivable, forcing people to move into places where they have not historically lived, and often where they are not welcomed. Reaching such a desperate state means these people have already experienced extreme suffering on many levels. The migration journey often leads to even more suffering. The struggle and tragic end for so many fleeing climate-driven economic and social conflicts is well documented in the news. It will get much worse as climate change unsettles far more people.

Migrants flowing into neighboring or distant countries often face exploitation and rejection by the occupants who feel unprepared or are unwilling to accommodate them. The fear of strangers can trigger hostility and lead to political upheaval that is often exploited by opportunistic politicians to grab power. The reflex is often to close the borders, roundup and deport migrants, and to blame those in power for not being strong enough on curbing migration. The burden of accommodating and absorbing large numbers of immigrants is significant. We all suffer from climate-driven migration.

Loss of Wealth and Financial Security

All of the negative consequence of our warming world will exact a direct cost on society. We already have many examples, as powerful storms, wildfires, floods, droughts, and rising seas destroy private property, and public infrastructure, and turn lives and entire communities upside down. History has shown that recovery from major disasters is in many aspects a mirage. What is lost is never truly recovered and the human toll extends well beyond the immediate years following these events. Areas with a high risk of disasters are now finding property insurance to be more expensive or unavailable. As insurers back away from communities or dramatically increase their rates, property values decline. And even when government steps in to provide some relief, the societal costs fall on all of us.

Our dependence on fossil fuels has driven enormous wealth inequality as we have transferred the wealth of the many and concentrated it in the hands of the wealthiest few. Nearly everywhere on Earth, including here in the United States, fossil fuel wealth is used to influence and control governments, and to ensure our continued dependence on fossil fuels. Collectively, we are poorer for it, while fossil fuel investors and fossil fuel revenue-dependent nations, like Russia, Iran, and Saudi Arabia, who manipulate the supply to keep prices high, continue accumulating more wealth. If we delay the transition to renewable energy, we will also delay our release from the yoke of the global fossil fuel industry.

Self-Destruction

The global fossil fuel industry is planning on strong demand for their products to continue through this century. On this course, humankind is facing a perilous future, made worse every passing day as we increasingly poison our atmosphere with fossil fuel emissions. No region on Earth will escape the devastating impacts of our overheated world. The toll in death, suffering, and destruction will fall on all of us, and especially on our descendants.

2 - AN ORDERLY TRANSITION

The party does not have to end, but the music might have to change.
– J.R. Rim, author, and popular quotist

Do Not Delay

If we do not act soon to eliminate our emissions from fossil fuels, we will experience a ruinous climate crisis this century. We already have the technology to transition to renewable energy well before 2050. This is no time to delay. We cannot afford to hold off utilizing what we already have in the hope of better technologies coming along. Every day delayed in the transition to renewable energy means more suffering.

Our tendency to resist change and to expect new technologies to solve our problems may delay the transition to renewable energy. Much of the hype about "miracle solutions" is seeded by fossil-fuel interests who want to delay the end of fossil fuel use. Exaggerated claims about the potential of carbon capture technologies, "natural" and methane-sourced hydrogen, and deceptive slogans like "Advancing Climate Solutions" (Exxon-Mobile) and "Renewable Energy Solutions" (Chevron) from fossil fuel suppliers while they invest in ever more fossil fuel reserves are examples of the "greenwashing" they use to polish their public image. These same companies have lied to us about the effects of burning fossil fuels for many decades.

Economic and Political Stability

The transition to renewable energy does not require us to experience unpredictable disruptions or unsettling changes. Because electrifying everything using renewable energy is less costly overall, more convenient, and better for our health and environment, change will be driven by choice as we become more aware of these advantages.

An important fact to appreciate is that as we use fossil fuels, we are transferring the economic damage caused by our emissions to everyone else the world over. Because carbon dioxide molecules stay in the atmosphere a very long time, these are costs we largely pass to future generations. Economists describe this as the Social Cost of Carbon (SCC). This measure estimates the present value of the economic damage of releasing carbon dioxide over the many years it will be in the atmosphere. This value is as much $.60 per pound of carbon dioxide [2]. To put this in perspective, it means burning one gallon of gasoline, that is responsible for releasing 25 pounds of carbon dioxide, represents a present value economic cost to global society of as much as $15. The person benefiting from using the gasoline pays a small out-of-pocket cost to buy the fuel while passing a significant cost to global society. Although imposing a tax or fee on fossil fuels has been proposed as a means for removing this economic distortion and to encourage reduced use of fossil fuels, it has so far failed the political test.

The fossil fuel industry has funded efforts to resist change and slow the renewable energy transition. Some of the most obvious examples are slowing the approval process for infrastructure improvements to connect renewable generation and energy storage projects to the electric grid. Any government agency controlled by people not friendly to renewable energy development can simply delay the needed approvals and permits. Many major projects have already been cancelled or significantly delayed using this tactic. Consumer choice does not easily overcome such hurdles, at least not until our votes remove those posing such barriers.

Government can play a role in overcoming the barriers. Providing incentives to encourage electrification of buildings, electric vehicle use, and to encourage electric vehicle fast-charger infrastructure are examples. Legislation and policies to fast-track new electricity transmission lines is another.

We will face many hurdles as we build out the renewable energy infrastructure. A well-planned transition will avoid energy disruptions by being certain that sufficient backup energy supply is available to cover extreme conditions. In addition, the political reality exists that compromise will always be needed to keep the renewable energy ball rolling forward. Situations will come up when this has the appearance of supporting continued use of fossil fuels. For example, here in the United States, we recently enacted groundbreaking renewable energy policies, while at the same time we produced more oil and natural gas than ever, largely to offset Russian energy disruptions to Europe and efforts by fossil fuel cartels to restrict their supply to keep prices high. Effective political leaders need to keep an eye on both local and global economic realities. They cannot help with change if they are not reelected.

Employment

The transition to renewable energy will create far more jobs than will be lost in fossil fuel related activities. That is of little consequence if your job will no longer be needed in the renewable energy powered world. Even if a person's skills and experience may be transferable to other industries, the new jobs may not be in the same location. Uprooting one's family is not always easy, especially if the property you own becomes depressed due to the demise of fossil fuel activities in the area.

Renewable-powered technology will alter the demand for some professions while also requiring many to learn new skills. For example, internal combustion vehicle technicians will experience reduced demand for their skills. Those who remain will need to be trained on electric vehicles. And some new car dealers, who have oversized political influence in most states, are threatened by the lower service and maintenance requirements of electric vehicles, and by companies like Tesla and Rivian who sell their electric vehicles direct to consumers. There will be many examples of jobs threatened or changed, new training requirements, changed ways of doing business, and relocations, all creating enough anxiety to make a lot of people fear the change to renewable energy. Fossil-fuel interests will continue to stoke this fear to block public support of renewable energy. Appeasing some of these fears will require government policies to provide retraining services, relocation incentives, and to encourage renewable technology manufacturing in communities where fossil-fuel related jobs will be lost.

Gradual Replacement of Fossil Fueled Equipment

We will not change all of our existing fossil fueled equipment at once. People vary in their tendency to embrace new technology. Some jump on the latest new gadgets, while others only after the experience of others prove positive. The majority of people fall in the middle, adopting to change slowly at first and then more rapidly as it becomes the new normal. And there are always some who resist until there is no choice. Cultural pressure and government policies can accelerate the process.

Much of the transition will occur gradually as equipment wears out. Some of the replacement will occur sooner because lower ongoing costs using renewable energy are sufficient to justify early retirement of the fossil fueled equipment. The early replacement of gas furnaces with heat pumps, especially for homes equipped with rooftop solar electricity, is a good example. The cost for electricity per unit of heat produced by the heat pump is lower than the cost for the same amount of heat from the old natural gas furnace. Over time the lower energy cost will pay for the heat pump. Electric vehicles offer a similar advantage with significantly lower energy and maintenance costs per mile driven.

Most residential and commercial property owners, and small businesses are not especially diligent about minimizing energy costs or emissions. Most tend to deal with their heating and cooking appliances as they fail and have no idea of their harmful emissions. Not having heat, air conditioning, or hot water often triggers an emergency reaction to fix it as soon as possible. We also tend to avoid a big upfront expense, regardless of long-term costs. Public education and informed repair technicians can help bring attention to the advantages of switching out gas appliances for a more efficient, safer, and earth-friendly electric alternatives. Because upgrading to heat pump water and space heaters often requires some additional electrical circuitry, it helps to be prepared for the needed upgrade before the emergency, or at least have a contractor who has an electrician that can respond on short notice. Rental property owners are starting to realize that lowering their tenants' energy costs and offering access to electric vehicle charging makes their property more desirable.

Although many businesses look more closely at overall long-term costs than do residential and commercial property owners, it does not always mean they will step up to fully electrify their facilities or vehicles. Sometimes they have short-term goals or investment priorities that get in the way. Over time, the lower overall costs of electrifying everything using renewably generated electricity will win out. Those who act sooner will benefit the most. When you encounter businesses that are oblivious to the advantages of utilizing renewable energy to power their operations, it should make you wonder what else they are ignoring.

Large businesses and institutions tend to look more closely at opportunities to lower their costs. Major technology companies such as Apple and Alphabet (i.e., Google) have been leaders in acting to lower their cost by taking advantage of renewable energy to power everything. Major education institutions, such as Columbia University and Stanford University, are among the many who have made great strides in adopting renewable energy. Even Walmart, a company well-known for cutting costs, is on track to achieving zero emissions from global operations by 2040. The same is happening throughout our economy, from heavy manufacturing, mining, shipping, retailing, and government. Wall Street is watching and rewarding companies with the foresight to transition to lower cost zero emission renewable energy.

An investment mentality is needed to recognize the advantage of renewable energy's lower overall cost. This is especially true where investment in existing fossil fueled equipment is both significant and has considerable remaining life. For example, writing off a fossil-fueled furnace that has another 10 years of life can be a difficult choice. But there is a simple formula. It is no different in principle than the choice millions of people have made as they transitioned to light emitting diode (LED) lighting. When they first became available, many people were reluctant to spend the extra money to replace their incandescent and florescent light bulbs. It took time for people to do the math of investing in higher upfront cost to benefit from significantly lower energy cost and far better reliability over time. Gradually the market for incandescent and florescent lighting has all but dried up because the math is in LED's favor. Installing solar panels or wind generation, investing in heat pumps for space and water heating, converting to an electric arc furnace to produce steel, or switching to electric vehicles, all require this sort of decision-making approach. Including the costs that fossil-fuel emissions impose on society should always be part of the math.

Business decisions by fossil-fuel suppliers and utilities will also be a factor as the transition to renewable energy continues. Aging infrastructure and reduced demand for fossil fuels will make some of their current activities unprofitable. For example, many of the aging natural gas distribution systems in the United States need to be replaced. This is an extremely expensive activity that will be paid for by utility ratepayers over the typical 50-year life of the pipes, plus a guaranteed profit for the utility. As utility customers transition to renewably powered electric heating and cooking, to both reduce their cost and eliminate their emissions, the remaining natural gas users will gradually pay an increasing share of the pipe replacement cost, eventually making the cost of natural gas prohibitively expensive. Neither the utility or the ratepayers will win in this scenario. It will be better for the ratepayers, the utility, and the climate to invest the funds to transition the entire area served by the aging natural gas pipe system to switch to electric heating and cooking. One approach to addressing this would be to offer financing programs to transition natural gas users to electric. Retail motor fuel distribution will also experience a gradual decline as the proportion of fossil fueled vehicles on our roads drops off. The number of retail gasoline stations will shrink as will the number of refineries. This will result in higher fuel cost, more inconvenience, and range anxiety for internal combustion vehicle drivers.

Building Infrastructure Takes Time

One of the most important factors limiting how fast the renewable energy transition will occur is how quickly our industries, electricity suppliers, and utilities can respond to affordably producing the required equipment and infrastructure. Electric vehicles are a good example. In 2020, the cost per kilowatt-hour (kWh) capacity for electric vehicle battery packs was about $155. In 2024, it dropped to $120. The cost is projected to fall to under $70 by 2030 [25]. At high volume with well-developed battery supply lines, electric vehicles will cost less to produce than internal combustion vehicles simply because they have fewer moving parts and are much easier to assemble. Having sufficient public fast-charging infrastructure is also crucial to achieving broad consumer acceptance of electric vehicles. Siting and outfitting the locations takes investment and time, and a power grid capable of supplying the electricity.

Public Support

The renewable energy transition will require public support across our entire economy. When the plumber gave me the "from another planet" look as I asked about replacing our natural gas water heater with electric,

I realized he was not up to speed on heat pumps or why anyone would want to stop emitting pollution and greenhouse gases. And sometimes a person's advice is influenced more by personal benefit than by the facts. If you ask for help from an auto salesperson who wants to sell you a gas-powered vehicle, it is not likely that an all-electric vehicles will be among their suggestions. Breaking through these knowledge barriers will take time.

Electricity Production

Transitioning to renewably generated electricity will require entirely different facilities of various types spread out over the landscape. The ownership structure of renewable electricity generation will be much less concentrated than has been the norm with fossil-fuel powered electricity. Renewable electricity can be generated wherever the sun shines, the wind blows, water flows, or there is intense heat.

Many residential, commercial, agricultural, and institutional properties with renewable electricity generation already exist. Large utility-scale renewable electricity generation and energy storage facilities will also be more common as major investors continue to trade in the deregulated electricity market. Instead of the revenue from electricity production going to a relatively small number of fossil-fuel suppliers and power plant operators, the profits and lower costs will be spread more broadly over the economy and closer to home.

Obstacles to building renewable electricity generation facilities remain. Solar arrays and wind turbines do alter the landscape. The "Not in my backyard" movement has taken hold in some areas, especially where fossil fuel interests exercise strong influence. Some jurisdictions have gone so far as to ban solar and wind farms. Where especially strong political polarization exists, support for renewable energy has become an ideological label. In the worst instances, people are reluctant to install solar or drive electric vehicles for fear of being ostracized or of having their property vandalized. Those who choose to reduce their energy cost and emissions should not have to face such intimidation.

Energy Storage

Electric utilities have always had reasons to store energy, not only for when their production of electricity exceeds demand, but also to draw from when demand exceeds their capacity to generate electricity. Because the sun does not always shine, and the wind does not always blow, renewable electricity generation is more intermittent than fossil fueled electricity generation. Our need for energy varies from day to day, by region, and by season. Reliably supplying our demand for electricity using renewable generation will require considerable energy storage capacity. Much of the intermittence of renewable electricity generation can be offset through geographically dispersed facilities and the ability to share electricity across great distances. During the hours when the sun is not shining in some places, it still may be shining brightly in others. Wind generated electricity is significantly more stable when drawn from across facilities over multiple regions for the same reasons.

As I am writing this on a sunny day in California, I am aware that more solar electricity is being generated across the State than we have demand for. Under these circumstances, the wholesale price of electricity drops to zero or even negative as those who have energy storage facilities soak up the extra supply for later use. Energy storage is already an important component of our electricity trading system that is seeing considerable new investment.

The oldest form of utility scale energy storage uses excess electricity to pump water into an elevated reservoir. Later when electricity is needed, these pumped-hydro storage facilities release water to generate electricity through a turbine generator. Chemical battery energy storage is seeing increasing use. This technology is easy to deploy and provides near instant response. Standalone residential and commercial installations as well as grid connected electric vehicles are already providing both grid storage and backup electricity during grid failures. And as local electric grids evolve into what are called *microgrids*, local energy generation and storage will be shared across the community to provide a more stable electricity supply.

Large energy storage facilities have an environmental impact. Water reservoir storage needs sufficient elevation for the water to fall, adequate water, and a connection to the electric grid. Former fossil fuel power plants are good sites for utility scale battery storage because of existing available space and electricity transmission lines. Development of energy storage infrastructure will need a supportive public.

Materials

Building renewable energy infrastructure will require a lot of new equipment and facilities. Unfortunately, fossil-fuel industry-funded disinformation campaigns have targeted this subject to create doubts either of our ability to find the needed materials or that our sourcing of the materials will catastrophically harm people and the environment. Electrifying everything will increase the need for metals such as iron, aluminum, copper, cobalt, and lithium. Although the Earth has ample supplies of these metals, and even the so-called rare-earth elements, new or expanded extraction operations will be needed to supply what will be required to fully transition the world to renewable energy. Avoiding harm to delicate ecosystems and to those nearby or working in these operations should always be a priority. We should insist on adequate regulation and transparency to ensure these protections are in place.

Extracting materials always has a negative impact on the environment. To maintain a balanced perspective, it is important to consider the harm to people and the environment from our use of fossil fuels. Fossil-fuel pollution has already caused an astonishing level of premature deaths, suffering, environmental damage, and economic harm. Fossil-fuel exploration, drilling, fracking, extracting, transporting, and processing activities have despoiled a staggering amount of the natural world. And continuing our large-scale use of fossil fuels will eventually yield an uninhabitable world. The transition to renewable energy will make a better world for all of us.

Recycling is an important factor that will minimize our need for more materials to build a renewable energy powered world. The natural motivation to recycle is clear when the retired equipment contains materials that are sufficient in value compared to the cost of collecting the retired equipment and of extracting the materials. There are plenty of examples where recycling is not taking place today. We should be working to force more of a circular economy where our environmental waste is minimized or even eliminated. There are also plenty of examples where recycling is working rather well. Large machines and their components, anything that contains significantly valuable materials, are routinely recycled–old automobiles, electric motors, appliances, furnaces, and now electric vehicle batteries and solar panels are among them.

Accelerating the Renewable Transition

We now live in a world powered primarily by fossil fuels. Most manufacturing, shipping, and mining operations now produce harmful air pollution and the greenhouse gas carbon dioxide. We are in the uncomfortable position of producing these harmful emissions as we manufacture the products needed for the transition to renewable energy. Eventually, when all our energy is renewably generated and all manufacturing, extraction, and transportation operations are renewably powered, we will no longer have this concern. Until then, how should this situation figure into the decisions we make about transitioning to renewable energy? Anything that delays the deployment of renewable energy infrastructure will also ensure that we experience more harmful effects from global warming and from the pollution produced as we continue to burn more fossil fuels. We cannot afford to delay!

3 - SOME IMPORTANT SCIENCE

We live in a society exquisitely dependent on science and technology, in which hardly anyone knows anything about science and technology.
– Carl Sagan, planetary scientist, and science communicator

Measuring Energy

As you explore how humankind will transition to a renewable energy powered world, you will need to understand how energy is measured, and how some technologies are more energy efficient than others.

To begin, all forms of energy, such as solar, heat, and electricity can be described in the standard unit of energy known as the joule (J). A single joule is not a lot of energy. Comparing it to the energy number we watch when dieting, one food calorie (i.e., kilocalorie) is equal to more than 4,000 joules. Electric energy is described using the watt (W), which is equal to one joule per second. One watt is abbreviated as 1 W. One thousand watts is described as one kilowatt, abbreviated as 1 kW, and equaling 1,000 joules per second.

Another measure of energy that describes the amount of accumulated energy, rather than the rate per second, is called *kilowatt hours*. Because there are 60 seconds per minute and 60 minutes per hour, an hour's worth of electric energy at a particular wattage level will equal a multiple of 3,600 (i.e., 60 × 60 = 3,600). One kilowatt-hour is abbreviated as 1 kWh, and equals 3,600,000 joules. The kWh is the familiar way utilities bill for electricity.

The kWh is also commonly used to describe an amount of energy even when the energy being described is not electricity. For example, an electric vehicle battery does not store electricity. It is storing chemical energy that can be used to produce electricity. This means that a battery charged to be capable of releasing 1 kWh of electricity will be storing enough chemical energy to produce 3,600,000 joules of electrical energy. Even the heat energy released from burning a fuel can be expressed in kWhs. Burning a gallon of gasoline releases 33.7 kWhs of energy (33.7 kWh × 3,600,000 J = 121,320,000 joules). This is the basis of the EPA miles per gallon equivalent (MPGe) rating on electric vehicles. Because the Tesla Model 3 can travel 3.95 miles per kWh, it earns a rating of 133 MPGe (i.e., 33.7 kWh / gallon × 3.95 miles / kWh = 133 miles / gallon equivalent).

Electrical devices and facilities that use or release electricity are rated at the maximum watts (i.e., joules per second) they can use or release. Equipment and facilities that deliver electricity from stored energy will be rated both by the maximum energy they can release per second, as well as how much they can provide in total. For example, the Ludington Michigan water reservoir and hydropower energy storage facility on the shore of Lake Michigan can deliver 19,548,000 kWhs of electricity and dispense it at a maximum rate of 2,172,000 kW, meaning it can deliver at this rate for 9 hours (i.e., 19,548,000 kWh / 2,172,000 kW = 9 hours).

Burning Fossil Fuels

The industrialized world has long lived with the harmful emissions from combustion (i.e., burning) of fossil fuels. As we explore the impact of these emissions, it is important to understand what is going on when fossil fuels are burned.

Fossil fuels, such as coal, oil, and natural gas, contain hydrocarbon molecules consisting of various combinations of hydrogen (H) and carbon (C). They also contain impurities such as sulfur (S), minerals, and metals like mercury (Hg), lead (Pb), iron (Fe), and others. The atmospheric air that is mixed in with fossil fuels as they are burned consists of a relatively uniform combination of gases that varies slightly depending on the amount of water vapor present. It contains 75% to 78% nitrogen (N), 20% to 21% oxygen (O), water (H_2O) vapor ranging from 0% to as much as 4%, and about 1% of other gases.

The combustion process starts with enough heat and pressure being applied to the fuel in the presence of oxygen to cause some carbon (C) and hydrogen (H) to break free from the hydrocarbon molecules and combine with oxygen (O) to form carbon dioxide (CO_2) and water (H_2O). This transition from unstable fuel molecules requiring high levels of internal energy to maintain their molecular structure, to stable carbon dioxide and water molecules requiring much lower levels of internal energy, results in the release of considerable heat energy. This heat causes a chain reaction to continue until insufficient fuel or oxygen remains.

Other than some ash and soot that may be left behind, we observe that the fuel is gone after it has burned. But all the elements within the fuel and air involved in the combustion process are still around, only now expelled into the atmosphere and combined very differently. In addition to the carbon dioxide (CO_2) and water (H_2O), many other molecules are released. These emissions include unburned hydrocarbons and carbon soot particles, smog producing nitric oxide (NO) and nitrogen dioxide (NO_2), nitrous oxide (N_2O), carbon monoxide (CO), sulfur dioxide (SO_2), and a variety of metal and ash particles.

Emissions also occur before fossil fuels are burned. Carbon dioxide and various hydrocarbons located underground with fossil-fuel deposits are released into the atmosphere as fossil fuels are extracted. As fossil fuels are distributed, processed, and stored even more hydrocarbons are released into the atmosphere. And all the fossil-fuel production activities that require energy, such as pumping, transporting, and refining are responsible for releasing emissions into the atmosphere. Even after the fuel is delivered to the end user, hydrocarbons from coal, crude oil, fuel oil, gasoline, diesel, and natural gas continue to be released. That smell of gasoline near a retail gasoline station is a good example of this leakage, as is that whiff of natural gas odorant you often detect as natural gas appliances ignite.

Lastly, secondary chemical reactions occur in the atmosphere from the molecules that are released from our use of fossil fuels. Ground level ozone (O_3), a molecule of three oxygen atoms, is a good example of this. This hazardous gas forms as oxides of nitrogen (NO and NO_2) interact with other smog molecules in sunlight. Another example is the formation of acid rain as atmospheric water and oxygen interact with sulfur dioxide (SO_2), nitrogen dioxide (NO_2), and carbon dioxide (CO_2) to produce sulfuric acid, nitric acid, and carbonic acid, respectively.

Warming from Greenhouse Gases

When solar radiation reaches Earth, about one-third of it strikes reflective surfaces in the atmosphere or on the Earth's surface, sending it back toward outer space. The remainder of this energy is either used to power natural processes like photosynthesis in plants, to produce electricity through solar panels, or is converted to heat energy.

The atmosphere contains various gases that, because of their molecular structure, interfere with the passage of heat (i.e., infrared energy) radiating from the Earth. Without this "greenhouse effect," heat would quickly pass to outer space leaving the Earth a frozen planet. Prior to the industrial revolution starting in 1750, our predecessors experienced relatively unchanging levels of greenhouse gases that had provided stable climate conditions. As we have increased the accumulated levels of greenhouse gases in our atmosphere, primarily from our use of fossil fuels, our climate has become increasingly warmer.

Although atmospheric water has a powerful heat trapping effect, it is not considered a cause of global warming. It is instead considered to be feedback from a warming world. As the atmosphere and surface waters warm, more water evaporates and the atmosphere holds more water.

The United States National Oceanic and Atmospheric Administration (NOAA) coordinates the Global Greenhouse Gas Reference Network consisting of 80 sampling locations around the globe that regularly measure the greenhouse gases [26]. Their annual analysis uses this information, along with the known warming qualities of each greenhouse gas, to determine the amount of heat retention averaged over the Earth's surface every second from the greenhouse gases. This is expressed as watts per square meter (W/m^2). The average warming from all tracked greenhouse gases in 1992 was 2.348 W/m^2 (2.348 joules per second/m^2). Ten years later it rose by 13% to 2.652 W/m^2. In 2012 it rose to 2.987 W/m^2, an increase of another 13%. Total greenhouse gas heating rose to 3.398 W/m^2 in 2022, a 14% increase.

Carbon Dioxide

Carbon dioxide (CO_2) molecules consist of one carbon and two oxygen atoms. In the atmosphere it is an invisible and odorless gas that is very long lived. Natural sources include volcanic activity, respiration from plants and other living organism as they combine carbon (C) and oxygen (O_2) to produce energy, and from combustion of organic matter containing carbon, such as wood and foliage. Other significant sources include the burning of fossil fuels and cement production.

Carbon dioxide is slowly drawn out of the atmosphere through photosynthesis as plants and some bacteria use solar energy to split water molecules to free hydrogen that is then synthesized with carbon dioxide to produce sugars. Carbon dioxide is also slowly absorbed into rock and surface waters, and falls to Earth as it combines with water and oxygen to produce carbonic acid rain.

The level of carbon dioxide (CO_2) in the atmosphere at the beginning of the industrial age in 1750 was 280 parts per million or .028% of the atmosphere. By 2022, the level increased 50% to 420 parts per million and was responsible for 64% of the warming (2.17 W/m^2) caused by the greenhouse gases. On our current business-as-usual course, atmospheric carbon dioxide will reach 550 parts per million by mid-century and continue climbing to more than 700 parts per million by 2100. In 2022 the global emissions of carbon dioxide from human activity weighed 81.144 trillion pounds (36.8 billion metric tons) [27].

Methane

The methane molecule, consisting of one carbon atom and four hydrogen atoms (CH_4), is an invisible and odorless gas that is the primary ingredient in natural gas. In 2022 methane was responsible for 19% of the warming (.65 W/m^2) caused by the greenhouse gases. The level in the atmosphere has increased nearly threefold since preindustrial times and has been increasing rapidly in recent decades. Significant amounts of methane leak into the atmosphere from fossil-fuel exploration, extraction, processing, and distribution operations, and from natural gas appliances. The other sources come from microbial decomposition of organic matter where there is little oxygen present. Soil and sediments hold enormous amounts of this biologic methane. Much of it is locked in frozen water crystals. Our warming oceans and atmosphere is causing more of this to be released. Water disturbed by large ships traveling near methane rich ocean sediments is also causing increased methane releases. Carbon dating of atmospheric methane reveals that about one-third is ancient fossil methane.

By mass methane is close to 100 times more potent as a heat trapping gas than carbon dioxide. Unlike carbon dioxide molecules that can stay in our atmosphere for a very long time, atmospheric methane breaks down in only about twelve years as the carbon combines with oxygen to form carbon dioxide and the hydrogen combines with oxygen to form water. Climate scientist sometimes describe methane's heat trapping capacity averaged over 100 years after it is released into the atmosphere as 20 times more potent than carbon dioxide.

Nitrous Oxide

Nitrous oxide, consisting of two nitrogen atoms and one oxygen atom (N_2O), was responsible for 6% of the warming ($.193$ W/m^2) caused by the greenhouse gases in 2022. Atmospheric nitrous oxide is formed during combustion of fossil fuels and through natural processes that break down nitrogen fertilizers.

Synthetic Greenhouse Gases

Various synthetic gases used as refrigerants and in industry were responsible for the remaining 11% of greenhouse gas warming ($.385$ W/m^2) in 2022.

Significant international efforts through the treaty known as The Montreal Protocol are underway to rein in synthetic gas emissions.

Reflection of Solar Radiation

Anything that reduces the solar radiation reflected back toward outer space will increase the Earth's temperature. Increasing solar reflection has a cooling effect.

Black Carbon Particulates

When carbon fuels are burned in our atmosphere some incomplete combustion occurs that produces tiny carbon soot particles. When these black carbon particulates encounter sunlight, as they float throughout our atmosphere and settle onto surfaces, they convert the solar energy to heat preventing any reflection of the solar radiation that would otherwise have taken place. The amount of atmospheric heating caused by black carbon (≈ 1.1 W/m^2) is near that caused by methane, nitrous oxide, and the synthetic gases combined, making it the second largest source of global warming after carbon dioxide [28].

Decreasing our emissions of black carbon produced from the burning of fossil fuels is one way that we may experience a noticeable climate cooling as our use of renewable energy becomes more dominate. Black carbon settles out of the atmospheric in a matter of weeks to months. Most of it is then quickly incorporated in the soil and oceans. There are other sources of atmospheric black carbon, such as wildfires. With ever hotter and dryer conditions, wildfires are larger and more common. This will offset some of the reduction of atmospheric black carbon particulates from ceasing our use of fossil fuels.

Clouds

As the Earth has warmed, the air currents flowing from hot equatorial regions toward the cooler poles have shifted. This has altered the global pattern of cloud formation with less highly reflective cloud cover near the equator. This feedback from our warming atmosphere has reduced the reflection of solar radiation causing yet more global warming.

Atmospheric Aerosols

Particles in the atmosphere that reflect sunlight have a cooling effect on our climate. Atmospheric particles also serve as nuclei of water droplets in the formation of clouds and influence how reflective the clouds are.

Sulfur Dioxide (SO_2) particles are released into the atmosphere from natural sources, such as volcanic eruptions, and from combustion of fuels containing sulfur. When combined with atmospheric water and oxygen they form liquid sulfate aerosols. These particles are highly reflective. Coal and some diesel fuels emit significant amounts of sulfur dioxide. The sulfate aerosols and clouds formed from this pollution have a cooling effect that masks the warming caused by greenhouse gases and black carbon. As the world has transitioned away from high sulfur fossil fuels, we have experienced less reflective sulfates in the atmosphere. With less solar reflection, we have also experienced increased solar energy production. [29]

Ice and Snow Cover

As snow- and ice-covered surfaces disappear from our warming planet, the amount of solar energy these surfaces reflect is reduced and the heat energy absorbed is increased. Not only is the added warming from this worsening as more reflective surfaces disappear, it is also a semi-permanent change that will not abate until global temperatures return to conditions that support the reestablishment of ice- and snow-covered regions and mountains.

Adaptation and Mitigation

Prior to the industrial revolution, natural processes had maintained a stable level of atmospheric carbon dioxide for many thousands of years. The 140 parts per million increase since then was produced primarily by burning fossil fuels that had been buried under the earth's surface for millions of years. The resulting increase in atmospheric carbon dioxide, weighing more than 1,000 billion tons (approximately 2,414,475 billion pounds or 1,095 billion metric tons), will not be quickly removed from the atmosphere by natural processes (see Extra Atmospheric Carbon Dioxide Exhibit). Failure to remove it by other means will cause us to live with the effects of global warming for centuries.

Although we may adapt and learn to live with some of the consequences of our warmer world, the natural world we want to preserve will not be saved without taking steps to restore global temperatures close to preindustrial levels. Otherwise, many of the changes global warming has set in motion will get progressively worse. For example, until glacial melting is stopped, sea level rise will continue until eventually raising the oceans by more than 200 feet (i.e., a twenty-story building).

The following sections address some additional factors that will influence how severe the worsening consequences will be from global warming, and also the pace of carbon dioxide drawdown that we may experience. How quickly we act to transition our global economy to renewable energy is the most important consideration. The slower the transition, the harsher the warming will be, and the slower the recovery. And if we delay too long, it is also possible that we will never achieve a more normal stabilized climate, at least not within the lives of immediately approaching generations. We must not delay!

Reducing Atmospheric Methane

Significantly reducing our methane emissions from our use of fossil fuels, waste disposal, and agriculture may provide opportunities to slow or reduce global warming. Fossil methane is produced over millions of years as organic matter buried deep underground is subjected to high pressure and temperature. If we stop using fossil fuels and plug the leaks of fossil methane from abandoned coal, natural gas, and oil extraction sites, the level of atmospheric fossil methane from these sources will drop quickly as it does not last very long in the atmosphere.

Biologic methane is formed from decomposition of organic matter by microorganisms known as methanogens. Unlike organisms that derive energy through respiration by combining oxygen (O_2) and carbon (C) to produce carbon dioxide (CO_2), these microbes derive energy by combining carbon (C) and hydrogen (H_4) to produce methane (CH_4). They live in environments where there is little free oxygen such as flooded rice fields, wetlands, water reservoirs, landfills, waste treatment plants, and animal digestive tracts.

Methane from landfills can be significantly reduced by directing organic waste to composting so that it will produce carbon dioxide instead. Another approach is to capture the landfill methane for use as a combustion fuel that will produce carbon dioxide which has a much lower heat trapping capacity in the atmosphere. Methane produced from collected animal waste on farms or waste treatment facilities can also be used for this purpose. It is impractical to gather waste from free roaming animals. The same is true of the flatulence and belched methane from ruminant animals, such as cows, bison, sheep, elk, deer, and goats. Although much of the world's population of wild animals has been decimated since the beginning of the industrial revolution, our need for food from a tenfold increase in human population since 1750 (from 800 million to 8 billion) is a primary driver of increased atmospheric methane.

Eating animal products is not an efficient source of nourishment. Nearly all the nutrition that goes into animal agriculture (more than 90%) is consumed by the animals and does not make it to our table. Transitioning to a more plant-based diet is not only healthier, it will also reduce the agricultural animal population resulting in less animal methane production, as well as the greenhouse gases from feed production, and to generate the energy used for pumping water, shelter, slaughter, processing, storage, and transportation.

The combined effects of these various approaches for reducing methane emissions could reduce global warming. This assumes that other events, such as methane escaping from melting permafrost soils, do not significantly add to the level of atmospheric methane. How quickly we act will determine how much we may slow the warming and restore our stable climate.

Engineering Solutions

A variety of engineering strategies to reduce the impacts of global warming are being evaluated. Some of these ideas are proposed by fossil-fuel interests who want to delay the transition to renewable energy. This makes no sense since we have many lower-cost and non-polluting solutions to replace fossil fuels. But some engineering strategies may be helpful to cool or stabilize our climate or to help us adapt. Diverting funding from the renewable energy transition for these engineering projects should always be evaluated relative to the cost, benefit, and likely success compared to the benefit from investing the funds to directly support the transition to renewable energy.

Atmospheric Solar Reflection Management: A commonly suggested engineering solution for lowering global temperature is the injection of reflective or cloud-producing particles into our atmosphere. Although sulfur dioxide could be used for this, it has the negative effect of producing acid rain. Other substances, such as sea salt particles, could also be used. Such an intervention would require a massive effort to have any meaningful effect. These efforts could also contribute to unpredictable and potentially undesirable weather. We need to learn a lot more before putting much into this approach.

Terrestrial Solar Reflection Management: Using light-reflecting colors on roofs, pavement, infrastructure, and even vehicles, would increase the amount of solar energy reflected back toward outer space. This can significantly lower the heat island effect in urban areas and help lower overall global temperature. And for underlying interior spaces, this also reduces the energy required for air conditioning. Even black synthetic fibers are adding to the heating. As researchers have analyzed the black carbon particles falling out of the atmosphere, polyester fibers are among them. The primary source is from automotive tire dust. Tires are made with rubber and synthetic fibers using an industrial pigment made from carbon called Carbon Black. They could just as easily be colored white, the natural color of latex rubber.

Greening Hot Places: Trees and other plants can have a significant local cooling effect. Plants accomplish this through transpiration as they draw water through their roots and release it through their foliage. The evaporation of the released water carries heat into the atmosphere. Although this reduces the heat in the local area, it does not cool the planet as it merely moves the heat around. Nonetheless, the local cooling can be lifesaving and there is some carbon sequestered in the plants. Making it work requires sufficient water. This can be a challenge in desert and drought prone areas. One technique that can be very effective is to engineer rain runoff so it is absorbed into the soil where the plants can access it throughout the year.

Carbon Capture: Capturing carbon dioxide and disposing of it so it will never be released into the atmosphere has been a commonly proposed engineering solution. Collecting carbon dioxide when it is concentrated is relatively easy. It becomes much more challenging when the carbon dioxide is mixed with other molecules, such as in a fossil-fuel exhaust stream with lots of water, a variety of pollutants, and many other elements are present. This is the approach fossil-fuel interests have frequently touted but never delivered, at least in an affordable and 100% effective form. Adding yet more cost to fossil-fuel energy production does not make economic sense when renewable energy is already lower cost. Direct air capture is an approach that is intended to draw down carbon dioxide from the atmosphere. With the current level of atmospheric carbon dioxide at 420 parts per million (.042%), 99.958% of the atmosphere is not carbon dioxide. It will require an enormous amount of energy to draw in enough air to gather and isolate a meaningful amount of carbon dioxide. It is worth doing the basic research to fully understand this approach. What to do with the captured carbon dioxide is yet another matter. It can be injected underground in some places, but not always with definitive assurance that it will stay there. And there are ways to break the carbon and oxygen bond to harvest pure carbon that could be buried or used in useful ways. This is a good area of fundamental research, but not a reason to delay the renewable energy transition.

Carbon Dioxide Absorption: A variety of techniques are being developed and tested for accelerating the natural absorption of carbon dioxide into ocean sediment and surface rock. These may prove to be useful for drawing down carbon dioxide.

Biochar Carbon Sequestration: When organic matter decomposes where oxygen is present, the carbon it contains ends up being combined with oxygen to form atmospheric carbon dioxide. If decomposition can be prevented, no carbon dioxide will be formed. Biochar consists of carbon and some ash produced by cooking biomass, such as ground-up wood, in a low oxygen environment. Depending on how deeply biochar is buried in soil, this stable form of carbon can forestall the formation of carbon dioxide from the carbon it contains for hundreds to many thousands of years. Large-scale biochar production may be a useful tool for drawing down atmospheric carbon dioxide. Because the weight of carbon dioxide consists of 27% carbon and 73% oxygen, one pound of carbon stored in biochar would be responsible for reducing atmospheric carbon dioxide by 3.7 pounds (1 pound / .27 = 3.7 pounds). It will take an enormous amount of biomass to sequester a meaningful amount of carbon in biochar. Biochar production does produce harmful air pollution.

Land, Ocean, and Agricultural Practices

Opportunities exist to reduce atmospheric greenhouse gases through land use, habitat restoration, and agricultural practices.

Land Re-wilding and Restoration: Our degradation of natural habitats has destroyed many places where carbon dioxide has been drawn from the atmosphere and stored. Restoring these places and saving those that remain can reduce atmospheric carbon dioxide over time. For example, forests are significant storehouses of carbon. Depending on species and conditions, a mature hardwood tree can sequester as much as 50 pounds of carbon dioxide per year [30] [31]. Over the past few centuries, much of our natural forestlands have been destroyed either for energy (firewood, dams, fossil-fuel extraction), building materials, agriculture, or to provide space for residential, commercial, industrial, or transportation infrastructure. Restoring forests with billions more trees will help ease the level of atmospheric carbon dioxide once we stop using fossil fuels. Because it takes about 20 years for a tree to reach maturity, it is not a fast response. With increasing wildfires, it may be difficult to stay ahead.

Aquatic Re-wilding and Restoration: Restoration and cultivation of aquatic plants, such as kelp and sea grass, can sequester large amounts of carbon dioxide. Microscopic phytoplankton is responsible for a major portion of the planet's photosynthesis and carbon sequestration. Warmer and more acidic water, loss of upwelling nutrients from shifting currents, and other climate change stressors are hampering phytoplankton growth. Bolstering the growth of these plants by restoring essential conditions and nutrients may provide an important means for drawing down carbon dioxide.

Regenerative Agriculture: How we produce food can have a big impact on the health of our ecosystems and how much carbon is stored in the soil. Soil biomass is a major storehouse of carbon. The most productive and sustainable soils contain a healthy mass of organisms and organic materials that help to retain water and protect from erosion. Agricultural plowing destroys this structure exposing the biomass to the atmosphere, causing carbon dioxide to be released into the atmosphere, and the loss of nutrient rich soil to wind and water erosion. No-till farming is an alternative to sod busting. Automated crop seeding is accomplished using no-till planting machines.

Control of Nitrogen Fertilizer: Over-use and poor control of synthetic and natural nitrogen fertilizers (i.e., animal waste) is a significant source of the potent greenhouse gas nitrous oxide.

Carbon Credits

Buying carbon credits can be an effective way to offset greenhouse gas emissions that you cannot yet avoid. The organizations that sell carbon credits invest in activities that remove greenhouse gases from the atmosphere or prevent greenhouse gas emissions. There have been some issues in this market with fraudulent carbon credits. Legitimate providers are "certified" to yield real and verifiable results, that are permanent, enforced, and additional, meaning they would not have happened anyway. Many organizations and individuals are buying carbon credits for both ongoing activities and special events, like plane trips. A typical annual subscription runs around $1 per 125 pounds of carbon dioxide. An offset for the typical 2,000 pounds of carbon dioxide emissions from 4,000 miles of commercial flight runs about $16. I use an organization that targets methane capture from landfills, farms, and abandoned coal mines.

4 - ELECTRICITY PRODUCTION

We are like tenant farmers chopping down the fence around our house for fuel when we should be using Nature's inexhaustible sources of energy–sun, wind and tide. I'd put my money on the sun and solar energy. What a source of power! – Thomas Edison, inventor, and businessman [32]

The solar radiation reaching Earth each hour is enough to supply all humankind's energy needs for an entire year [33]. The force of wind is a vast untapped source of energy. Where water is moving, be it falling, in a current, in a tidal flow, or wave, there is energy to be captured. And from the heat all around us in the air and land, and from deep below the Earth's surface, there is inexhaustible energy to be utilized. We have the technology to draw upon all these sources to transition to a renewable energy powered world.

Electricity Demand In 2050

Electrifying everything by 2050 will mean keeping up with the needs of our growing population and economy, and a warmer world. Generating the added electricity to power the equipment that will replace fossil fueled machinery used in transportation, manufacturing, agriculture, heating, cooking, and other activities will further increase the demand for electricity. Powering these activities with efficient electric solutions will use much less energy than the fossil fueled equipment they will replace. For example, internal combustion engines are not efficient, utilizing less than 20% of the energy released during combustion to perform work. Electric vehicles use as little as one-fifth the energy per mile driven as a gasoline powered vehicle. Heat pump furnaces and water heaters require less than one-third the energy of natural gas-powered units. And electric induction cooktops use much less energy than gas or conventional electric units.

Research that takes all these factors into consideration estimates that by 2050, an all-renewable energy powered United States will have end use electricity demand of 8.25 trillion kWhs [1]. This is about double the 4.05 trillion kWhs of end use demand we had in 2022 [34]. We have experienced significant electricity demand increases in the past. In 2022, it was double what it had been 40 years before in 1982, and 14 times greater than it had been in 1950. Because of such low cost, new electricity generation is already dominated by renewable energy investments. As old fossil fueled power plants are retired, they are being replaced by renewable generation and energy storage for the same reasons. And in many instances, fossil fueled power plants will be retired early, motivated by lower renewable energy cost and the urgency to eliminate fossil fuel emissions.

Solar

Photovoltaic Solar Panels

The photovoltaic effect was first documented by Edmond Becquerel in 1839. His discovery described an electric current generated when sunlight strikes certain semiconductor materials. During the last 50+ years this technology has been refined and commercialized. The typical residential rooftop solar panel installed in the United States today will produce just over 500 kWhs of electricity per year at a cost of less than $.09 per kWh based on a 25-year depreciation of the average $1,000 solar panel. For a point of reference, 500 kWhs is enough electricity to power a Tesla Model 3 about 2,000 miles at a cost of under $.025 per mile, a small fraction of what it would cost to power any gasoline powered automobile. Although the effective cost of solar electricity varies depending on the rate credited by the utility for excess solar generated electricity that is exported to the grid, it generally remains much lower than buying electricity from the utility. Large commercial and utility scale solar arrays produce electricity at under $.04 per kWh [35], less than one-half that of home solar.

Home and commercial building solar panel electricity production will continue to grow as more people become familiar with the savings available to them. Utility scale solar panel electricity production is also on the rise, as more investors become players in the energy trading market.

Floating solar arrays on water reservoirs, small lakes, and irrigation canals are becoming more common. They are easy to install, many reservoirs have direct access to electric transmission lines, and they have the added benefit of reducing water evaporation.

New lightweight solar panels are making it possible for many buildings that could not support the weight of traditional panels to install solar arrays. And thin flexible solar panels are finding all sorts of applications, like on camper trailers and even in the skin of electric vehicles.

Agrivoltaics is an emerging practice where solar panels are used in agricultural settings to produce electricity while also improving crop production. This is accomplished by optimizing the light energy reaching the plants, by reducing water evaporation, and by protecting crops from damaging weather conditions. Agrivoltaics is especially effective in hot climates.

Parking lots are proving to be great locations for solar arrays. Not only do they integrate well with electric vehicle charging, they turn these environments into comfortable sheltered spaces. People love them!

Solar panels have been leading the way for low-cost renewable electricity generation. They are easy to install, reliable, effective throughout the lower 48 states and Hawaii, and require little extensive site improvements or maintenance. Utility scale solar panel electric generation is now lower cost than fossil fuel powered generation. Because of this versatility and low cost, solar panels will likely provide close to 50% of our electricity generation in 2050 [1].

There has been a lot of disinformation circulating about solar panels taking an unreasonable amount of space. A simple math exercise is useful to dispel this misrepresentation. If 2050 annual end use electricity demand is expected to be 8.25 trillion kWhs, and if one-half is from solar panels, that would equal 4.125 trillion kWhs. Allowing for a 20% loss from energy storage and transmission of electricity, the required electricity generation from solar panels would equal 5 trillion kWhs. Today's average rooftop solar panels in the lower 48 states produce 500 kWhs per year and measures about 17.6 square feet. With the land area of the lower 48 states at 3.12 million square miles, it works out to only .2% of the land area will be required for solar panels (See LAND AREA FOR SOLAR Exhibit). Because much of it will be installed over existing utilized spaces, the area devoted exclusively to solar arrays will be much less.

Concentrated Solar

Concentrated solar electricity generation uses focused mirrors to generate extreme heat that can be used to produce electricity through a steam generator. These are large utility scale facilities, typically located well away from population centers such as the Ivanpah, California complex in the Mojave Desert. They also include significant heat storage using molten salts to allow for continued steam turbine powered electricity generation long after the sun goes down. They come in two basic designs. The tower design focuses sunlight on a central heating tower. The other design uses parabolic mirrors that focus the light on an oil-filled pipe passing directly in front of the mirrors. The pipe runs from mirror to mirror adding heat on the way to the steam generator. The parabolic design is newer and there is little available information about them in terms of cost, reliability, and productivity.

Concentrated solar's ability to produce large amounts of energy during daylight and well after sundown has been attractive to investors. It is most productive between 40 degrees north and south of the equator. The north 40-degree line in North America runs approximately through Reno, NV, and Philadelphia, PA.

With concentrated solar electricity production now costing more than solar panel electricity production, the future prospects for concentrated solar are uncertain.

Wind

Many regions on the globe experience consistently strong winds. The United States has sufficient wind generation capacity to supply all our electricity needs. But wind generation is not welcome everywhere. The public often objects to the presence of large wind turbines for appearance and noise reasons. The newest designs are located to avoid predictable bird flight paths and utilize technology that significantly reduce bird and bat collisions with the turbine blades.

A newly emerging segment of this industry supplies small wind generators. They include scaled down traditional shaped wind turbines and a variety of designs intended for urban settings that are unobtrusive, and safer for birds. They have not yet taken hold in urban areas to the extent of residential solar, but are finding buyers, especially in rural areas.

Wind-powered electricity generation is now lower cost than fossil fuel powered generation. Wind turbines are expected to provide about as much electricity as solar by 2050 [1].

Land-Based Wind Turbines

Large-scale wind farm electricity generation began in the United States in the 1970s. Since then, they have steadily increased in number, as have their size and production per turbine. Generation capacity of the average wind turbine put in service in 2020, was 10,116,000 kWhs per year, equaling the generation of approximately 20,232 residential solar panels (US EIA). Land-based wind turbine technology is mature. Placement based on known available wind energy in a location now provide accurate predictions of production, reliability, and life expectancy. This sort of certainty is of course important to investors.

North America has vast areas with exceptionally good wind capacity that are not yet developed. Many projects are on hold awaiting permitting and local approvals, while others are simply lacking a grid connection to transmit the electricity. Politicians opposing renewable energy development are often a factor in both types of roadblocks. Cost of land-based wind generated electricity was under $.04 per kWh in 2022 [35].

Ocean-Based Wind Turbines

Many areas along our coasts have strong persistent winds. On our east and gulf coasts, where nearshore ocean depths are not great, wind turbines will be mounted on the seafloor. Where ocean depths are much greater, such as on our west coast, they will be installed on floating platforms that are tethered to the ocean floor. Underwater transmission lines deliver the electricity to shore. Most of these large turbines will be sited well off shore beyond the horizon from land. Like land-based wind generation, offshore wind potential is enormous. As these new installations prove successful, we will likely see much more investment.

Water

Hydroelectric

Electricity generation from hydroelectric dams has been around for more than 100 years. Many of the older dams have silted up and are no longer productive. And many others are experiencing low water levels from drought or overdrawing from their source waters. Some of the biggest facilities like Grand Coulee Dam in Oregon and Robert Moses Niagara Hydroelectric Power Station in New York will be around for a long time. Major new dam construction is not expected to provide much of our increased electricity generation in coming years. They are expensive, take a long time to build, have an enormous carbon footprint, and often destroy prized natural resources and sacred sites. We will likely see more dams coming down than going up.

Small-scale hydroelectric electricity generation is seeing some growth. They utilize fish-safe water turbines placed in existing flowing streams and small rivers, and even in sewage treatment plants and industrial operations where water is flowing with enough force to generate electricity. They connect to the grid much like home solar, providing electricity for private use with the excess going on to the grid for use by the local utility.

All hydroelectric electricity generation will likely account for about 4% of total electricity production in 2050 [1].

Currents

Powerful and consistent currents operate below the ocean surface. Placing a large turbine in such a flow has great potential for generating electricity. Many challenges exist. Finding a location close enough to run underwater transmission lines is one. This is a relatively new technology that is seeing some investment. The potential for supplying affordable electricity to the United States from ocean currents is uncertain.

Tidal

Many near ocean locations have significant tidal flows that can be used to generate electricity by either placing turbines in the flow of water, such as through a channel where the tide flows, or by generating electricity and sequestering the high tidal water in a reservoir as it flows in, and then generating electricity as the water is released back into the ocean as the tide lowers. Because tides are highly predictable, this source of electricity can help stabilize intermittent sources. Although many locations in the northern hemisphere have significant tidal flows, most are outside of the United States. This is not new technology. The La Rance Tidal Power Station has been in operation since 1966 in Brittany, France. Tidal flows in many rivers have also been tapped in recent years with good success. This activity is relatively new to the United States and has yet to be established as a significant and affordable source of electricity. As with water current electricity generation, the potential of tidal generation in the United States is uncertain.

Wave

Ocean waves hold a tremendous amount of energy. Capturing this energy to produce electricity has taken several forms. One uses the force of waves as they reach the shore to move a mechanical device that generates electricity. Some of these are already in use in Europe where especially strong waves crash ashore. The other approach is to use the rise and fall of waves to generate electricity off shore. There are several designs that are in early stages of development. There is certainly a lot of potential for wave generation, though it has yet to demonstrate how productive, reliable, and cost effective it can be.

Geothermal

Near Surface

Areas with intense heat near the surface have long been used to produce steam to power generators. One of the largest is in the Mayacamas Mountains in Northern California consisting of 22 facilities spanning an area of 30 square miles. The small number of sites with intense near-surface volcanic heat limits the potential of this technology.

Deep Drilling

A new geothermal approach under development uses deep drilling technology from the oil and gas industry to drill deep enough to reach temperatures capable of producing steam to generate electricity. Everywhere on Earth, the deeper we drill the hotter it gets. If this proves to be effective and economical, it could open geothermal electricity generation for use in far more locations. There is still much to be learned about this approach.

Nuclear

The United States has about 90 nuclear powered electricity generation reactors in operation. Many are nearing the end of their useful life and will be decommissioned in the next few decades. The good side of nuclear power is that it reliably produces a lot of electricity while producing no smoke or greenhouse gas emissions. On the bad side, they are exceedingly expensive and time-consuming to build, expensive to maintain, have oversized imbedded greenhouse gas content, produce radioactive waste that we have not found places to safely store away, pose some risk of nuclear meltdown, and require mining and processing of nuclear fuels that are harmful to the people living nearby or handling the material.

Our latest new nuclear plant to go online went into service in March 2024 in Georgia. The twin reactor facility took 12 years to construct at a cost of $34 billion. It has an expected life of 60 years with annual electricity production expected to be about 20 billion kWhs. During the construction period, the cost of solar went down considerably and their efficiency went up. In the words of Mark Woodall of the Sierra Club of Georgia "customers would have been better off with more solar and battery storage than with two exorbitantly expensive nuclear reactors." [36]. It is a valid argument. Not only would comparable solar generated electricity cost less, it would have been accomplished long before twelve years, eliminating the fossil fuel power plant emissions that occurred while waiting on completion of the nuclear plant construction, and the greenhouse gas emissions from constructing the reactors. The region surrounding this site will be exposed to some risk of nuclear accident while also becoming a semi-permanent storage area of nuclear waste. As the existing nuclear powered electric generation reactors are retired, there will not likely be new large-scale facilities built to replace them.

The prospect exists for small scale lower cost nuclear reactors. Several well-funded startups are researching and developing designs that may prove to be safe and more affordable. For now, the urgency of the climate crisis tells us to move forward with the low-cost renewable technology we now have, solar and wind with energy storage.

The Water Cost of Generating Electricity

Fossil fuel exploration, extraction, and processing uses a significant amount of water in drilling, fracking, mining, refining, and coal handling operations. Uranium mining and processing for nuclear power plants also uses and contaminates a lot of water. Fossil fuel, nuclear, and geothermal electricity generation plants also use enormous amounts of water for steam generation and evaporative cooling.

On average, each kWh of electricity generated in the U.S has used about 12 gallons of water [37]. For the average household that uses about 30 kWhs per day [38], that amounts to 360 gallons of water EVERY DAY! This has a significant societal cost, and in dry climates especially serious environmental consequences. Because solar panel and wind turbine electricity generation does not require any steam or cooling water, transitioning to these sources of electricity will free up an enormous amount of water for other uses [39].

2050 Electric Generation Mix

Many mixtures of electricity generation will be possible in 2050. The most likely mix will have solar at 47%, wind about the same, hydroelectric at 4%, and all others at 2% [1]. Although wave, tidal, ocean current, geothermal, and small nuclear have potential, they are not well developed and are not expected to make a significant contribution in the United States during this time frame. The low cost of solar and wind generated electricity, which is still dropping, is driving their dominance. We must not delay!

5 - STORING ENERGY

Energy cannot be created or destroyed; it can only be changed from one form to another. – Albert Einstein, theoretical physicist

Energy storage is not unique to the renewable energy revolution. The carbohydrates we metabolize to power our bodies is stored energy, as are fossil fuels. Electric utilities have always had good reasons to use electricity to store energy that could later be used to generate electricity. This allows for alternate electricity generation during planned maintenance of power plants and to handle peeks in demand above the capacity of power stations. Because of the intermittent nature of wind and solar, considerable energy storage will be needed in a 100% renewable energy powered world.

Chemical Batteries

With the growing use of electric vehicles, large rechargeable battery packs are now commonplace. They are called chemical batteries because the energy they store utilizes electrochemical cells to store chemical energy that is used to produce electricity. Electrochemical cells require metals to support the chemical reaction. Lightweight lithium is the primary metal of choice for electric vehicle batteries. Lithium-ion batteries are used for a wide variety of other mobile applications from cell phones to lawn mowers. Because this technology is mature and readily available, and offers near instant charge and discharge performance with very high efficiency and long life, they are also being used in stationary energy storage applications, such as for residential energy storage and backup. Excess grid electricity is used to store energy in batteries to later generate electricity when renewable energy production fluctuates. This will be increasingly common as renewable energy becomes more widely used.

There are other chemical battery designs being developed and deployed. Georgia Power has a large chemical battery energy storage facility that utilizes iron-air battery technology. Although this chemistry is not as efficient as lithium-ion, they estimate the cost per kWh stored is about one-fifth [40]. Sodium-ion and vanadium flow batteries also showing a lot of promise. Time will tell if these or other designs become widely used. For the immediate future, we can expect to see much more use of lithium-ion batteries.

Gravity Batteries

Gravity batteries use a lifted mass to create potential energy based on the lifted height and force of gravity acting upon the mass. Electricity is generated when the mass is lowered. The physical requirements of gravity batteries are very different than chemical batteries. A typical 10 kWh lithium-ion residential backup battery pack that is mounted on a garage or exterior wall weighs about 100 lbs. Achieving the same 10 kWhs of potential energy with a gravity battery lifting to a height of 1,000 feet will require a mass weighing about 28,000 pounds. Lifting the mass only 500 feet will require twice as much weight. These are large facilities.

Pumped Hydro

Pumped hydroelectric gravity batteries use electricity to pump water into an elevated reservoir. When electricity is needed, water is released to fall through a water turbine to power a generator. This is the same technology used in hydroelectric generation with the added step of pumping the water into a reservoir.

Two types of pumped hydro systems exist:

- Open-loop systems pump the water up into the reservoir from a nearby natural body of water, such as a lake, ocean, or river.
- Closed-loop systems have a lower reservoir where the water is pumped from, and an upper reservoir where water is stored until it is released back into the lower reservoir to generate electricity. Closed loop systems do need to have an available source of water to initially fill the reservoir and to compensate for evaporation and leakage.

One of the largest open-loop pumped hydro energy storage facilities went into service in Ludington, Michigan in 1973. It draws and returns water to Lake Michigan. A good example of a large closed loop system is the Helms Hydroelectric Energy Storage Facility in the Sierra Nevada Mountains east of Fresno, California. It has been in service since 1984. Consisting of the upper Courtright and the lower Wishon reservoirs, it draws replenishment water from the Kings River. There are many different closed-loop designs. One or both reservoirs can be underground using caverns or old mines. Underground reservoirs benefit from lower evaporation and are better protected from freezing.

Pumped hydro is and will likely continue to be the largest source of long-duration stored energy globally. The technology is mature and provides relatively good response times to generate electricity while returning about 80% of the electricity used to pump the water. The United States Department of Energy National Renewable Energy Laboratory has identified nearly 12,000 desirable sites for new large-scale closed-loop pumped storage facilities in the contiguous 48 United States [41].

Lifted Solid Mass

Lifted solid mass gravity batteries are mechanical devices that lift heavy weights using an electric motor powered by excess electricity. The process is reversed to generate electricity as the mass is lowered. There are several designs. One uses an automated crane to lift and stack heavy blocks. Another raises heavy containers within a structure of shafts, similar to elevator shafts.

Not requiring a water supply is one of the advantages of solid mass gravity batteries. Once the design is perfected, duplicates can be produced and constructed quickly. Several companies have them in development and are gaining valuable experience about their reliability and cost of operation. Preliminary claims of over 80% efficiency are encouraging. Skyscrapers are already being designed with internal lifted solid mass energy storage.

Compressed Gas Energy Storage

Compressed air has long been used to store energy and to power mechanical devices. Use of pneumatic tools, like those used to remove and install automotive wheels, is a common example of this. Utility-scale compressed air storage can be used to store large amounts of energy. One of the oldest examples built to generate electricity has been in operation for more than 20 years in Huntorf, Germany. Compressed carbon dioxide is also being used to store large amounts of energy for generating electricity. Utility-scale compressed gas storage facilities are now emerging as a reliable energy storage approach that does not require large amounts of water, or significant amounts of greenhouse gas emissions to build.

Hydrogen Energy Storage

Hydrogen is often touted as an ideal portable energy storage medium. When pure hydrogen is used to produce electricity through a fuel cell, the only emission is water and heat. This makes it sound like a perfect solution to our energy storage needs. The reality is that making use of hydrogen is challenging.

Because hydrogen readily combines with oxygen to form water, there is little free hydrogen on Earth. There are some geologic conditions that can produce hydrogen, although little is known about the amount available or how to effectively extract it. Deposits of this "Natural Hydrogen" may someday prove to be a useful source. Most of the hydrogen that is produced today comes from methane (CH_4) using a process called *steam reforming* that separates the hydrogen from methane while releasing significant amounts of carbon dioxide. This "Grey Hydrogen" process requires a lot of energy to produce the steam that is typically powered by fossil fuels that also release a lot of carbon dioxide. It should come as no surprise that fossil fuel companies are touting hydrogen because they see it as a market for their hydrocarbons. Some are proposing the use of carbon dioxide capture and storage technologies to clean up the process, what they are calling "Blue Hydrogen," which also requires a lot of energy. Using hydrocarbons to produce hydrogen does not solve our carbon dioxide problem. The other source for hydrogen is to use electricity through a process called *electrolysis* to separate hydrogen from oxygen in water molecules. When powered by renewably generated electricity, electrolysis produces "Green Hydrogen" that has no carbon dioxide emissions, only water and waste heat. If we are to use hydrogen, electrolysis is the way to produce it.

The efficiency of electrolysis varies from 70% to 80%, meaning between 30% and 20% of the energy used is lost as waste heat. Compressing hydrogen gas, which is required for storage and transport, uses about one-third of the energy the hydrogen contains. And hydrogen fuel cells lose between 40% and 60% of the energy as waste heat when they generate electricity. This means the overall cycle from electrolysis, through compression and fuel cell electricity generation, is between 22% and 38% efficient. If you use 100 kWhs of electricity to produce hydrogen, what you get back when the fuel cell produces electricity is between 22 kWhs and 38 kWhs. Powering a vehicle with hydrogen fuel cells will use three to four times the electricity of a chemical battery-powered vehicle. Using the hydrogen as a fuel for internal combustion engines is even less efficient and will also produce harmful oxides of nitrogen (NO and NO_2).

The challenges with hydrogen do not stop there. Sourcing and purifying the water used for electrolysis uses some energy. Storing and distributing hydrogen uses yet more. As the smallest of all molecules, hydrogen (H_2) is especially difficult to contain. Specialized and expensive storage tanks, pipes, hoses, fittings, and couplers are required to prevent this combustible fuel from quickly escaping into the atmosphere where it will readily burn if exposed to an ignition source. When hydrogen burns in daylight, the pale blue flame is nearly invisible making it difficult to detect. Hydrogen leaking into the atmosphere also slows the breakdown of ground level ozone and atmospheric methane.

There may be several roles for hydrogen to play in the renewable energy future. Aviation will likely utilize hydrogen, either directly as a fuel or as a component in the manufacture of carbon neutral combustion fuel. Chemical battery-powered class eight commercial vehicles–those tractors we see pulling large trailers on our highways–require large battery packs that are not only heavy, reducing the load the vehicle can carry, but they take some time to recharge. Because hydrogen refueling can be accomplished more quickly, hydrogen fuel cell power may prove to be viable for some of these long-haul applications. It may also be useful to power locomotives and large ocean-going ships.

Because green hydrogen can be produced anywhere there is renewable electricity and water, it will likely serve as a transportation fuel for some applications that need fuel in widely dispersed locations. And hydrogen may also play a part in supplying grid energy storage. The inefficiency of hydrogen energy storage is not so important when the electricity used to produce the hydrogen is so abundant that it is free or even negative. As the price of renewable electricity, hydrogen production, and fuel cell equipment falls, we may someday find hydrogen energy storage to be affordable and practical. This technology has promise, but a long way yet to go.

Flywheel Energy Storage

Flywheels have long been used in internal combustion engines to reduce vibration. The mass and rotational speed of the flywheel determines the rotational energy stored. Electric utilities are using sophisticated flywheels to stabilize electricity supplies. These are large high-tech devices. The perfectly balanced heavy flywheel and motor-generator rotor assembly is encased within a vacuum chamber and levitated using a magnetic bearing that allows it to rotate with minimal friction. Once it is spun up to speed, it requires very little energy to maintain speed. Should the electricity supply suddenly drop, the flywheel motor switches to generator mode to make up the difference, allowing time for other electricity sources to be deployed. The flywheel stabilizes electricity supply.

Thermal Energy Storage

The ground below us and the atmosphere around us act as massive thermal batteries. Low temperature thermal batteries are commonly used for space and water heating and cooling. Any substance that can store heat or cold can be used. One of the most common is the relatively stable temperature below ground. Ground source electric heat pump heating and air conditioning systems absorb heat that is stored underground to provide interior heat. When in air conditioning mode, they release heat absorbed from the interior space into the ground. These systems are used in colder climates. Air source electric heat pump heating and air conditioning systems operate in the same manner; except they simply use the ambient air outside the structure as the thermal battery. Air source systems are effective in climates common through most of the United States.

Water heaters with standing water storage are thermal batteries. The heat can be from sunlight, or from a heat source such as an electric heat pump, electric resistance heating coil, or from waste heat from other processes. Water coolers with liquid water or ice storage are also thermal batteries. The cooling is typically provided through electric refrigeration (i.e., heat pump). Buildings and district heating and cooling systems serving large campuses, industrial sites, military bases, and major sections of many cities are heated and cooled through thermal batteries that pump heated and cooled water throughout the system.

Sand and soil batteries, either in the ground or in above-ground containers, can provide heating throughout the winter using heat that is produced from renewable energy sources. Such systems are in use in Scandinavia. High-temperature thermal batteries using molten salt are in use at concentrated solar plants to store large amounts of heat to power steam-generated electricity when the sun is not shining.

We will make extensive use of both natural and manmade thermal batteries as we transition away from fossil fuels.

2050 Energy Storage Mix

Chemical battery and flywheel energy storage will dominate the rapid response short- and medium- duration applications for electricity generation from energy storage. Pumped hydro will continue to supply the most energy storage for long-duration electricity generation, complimented by compressed gas, lifted solid mass, and perhaps some green hydrogen. Ground and air sourced thermal energy storage will be our "go to" source for heating.

Land use for renewable energy generation and energy storage will be significantly less than the land area currently occupied by fossil-fuel infrastructure and fossil-fueled electricity generation [1].

6 - ELECTRICITY DISTRIBUTION

This is our grid in a nutshell: it is a complex just-in-time system for making, and almost instantaneously delivering, a standardized electrical current everywhere at once. – Gretchen Bakke, cultural anthropologist

Microgrids

Conventional electric utility systems used centralized generation plants with electricity distributed through a grid of conducting cables connecting to end users. Although they used electricity produced from multiple power plants and from sources outside the utility, they did not have customers providing electricity to their systems. This all changed with the deployment of residential solar panels and wind turbine electricity generation. Not only did this mean some customers would be buying less electricity from the utility, the utility would also have to manage the electricity added to the grid from these sources.

Now with many utility customers installing their own energy storage and even more generation capacity, the traditional local grid is starting to morph into a microgrid with some individual users and sections of the grid capable of operating autonomously, at least some of the time. Local energy storage also reduces the stress on the greater grid, as it buffers peak period demand using locally generated and stored energy. Making this a reality everywhere will require a smart grid where electricity sources can be managed to supply power across the microgrid. As microgrids evolve, large area power outages will be less likely because of the pooled electricity stored and generated locally.

You may be wondering if we need electric utilities. Although there are some people living all-electric and off-grid, at our latitude the amount of personal long-term energy storage required to make it through our long winter is usually cost prohibitive. Having oversized personal solar, wind or hydroelectric generation can make it possible for some to power through winter off-grid, but typically not without a lot of compromises.

Electricity Utilities

Electricity utilities are regulated by the states. Their financial structures include investor, public, and cooperative ownership. Most utility consumers in the United States are served by investor-owned for-profit utilities that are overseen by public utility commissions. How commissioners are assigned varies by state, some being appointed by governors, some by legislatures, or elected. Investor-owned utilities operate under rules that guarantee them a set return percentage on invested capital. This tends to encourage them to invest capital. Commissioners are responsible for approving capital investments to ensure it is the lowest cost alternative, approving contracts for energy sourcing, seeing that state laws and energy goals are followed, and monitoring the prices customers are charged for energy and services.

Politics sometimes influence utility commission decisions. In states where fossil-fuel interests exercise great power, utilities have often favored continuing with fossil fuels. With the price of solar and wind now lower than fossil fuels, this is becoming harder to justify. Commissioners are often close to the utilities they oversee, either from prior work experience, or other personal interests. This can color their decisions. We have seen states with excellent solar and/or wind exposure perpetuating fossil fuel electricity generation and discouraging renewable energy production and storage. There have also been instances when electricity producers have attempted to limit competition by discouraging consumers from installing solar panels and wind turbines. Transparency and public activism are important to keep utilities working for the best interest of the public.

North American Electric Grid

Utilities have power lines that connect with other nearby utilities and other areas of their own operations to share electricity. Such grid networks must be managed to balance electricity generation and demand load. This requires them to control electricity supplied from generation facilities, electricity drawn from or sent to other utilities, and to send excess electricity to energy storage facilities. Making the best use of renewable energy generation and storage will require more connections with nearby, regional, and even distant electricity suppliers. Without a wide network of interconnecting electricity transmission lines, we are not currently equipped to support widespread energy sharing across the United States or all of North America.

As large-scale renewable electricity generation facilities integrate into a broad network of interconnected electricity suppliers, the barriers to a continent-wide energy trading network will fall, allowing electricity to flow from where it is abundant and lowest cost. Sending electricity over great distances does come with the cost of energy loss from the heat produced as the electricity flows through the wires. Today's most efficient high-voltage direct current technology loses just over .5% per 100 miles. With such low energy loss, there is significant potential for taking advantage of electricity generated anywhere in North America.

Overall, our electricity distribution system will need to be hardened to withstand the worsening weather extremes, and upgraded to support the doubling of electricity demand. This does not mean every component of our grid will need to be doubled. For example, the capacity of our 100-year-old design steel core high-voltage transmission lines can be doubled merely by upgrading to lighter carbon fiber core conductors. We have the technology and resources to do all of this.

7 - ELECTRIFYING EVERYTHING

Change is the law of life. And those who look only to the past or present are certain to miss the future. – John F. Kennedy, 35th President of the United States

Taking Action to Eliminate Fossil Fuel Emissions

The mix of fossil fuel greenhouse gas sources varies widely around the world. In the United States, our personal transportation and households represent less than one-half of our total emissions. Most of our emissions come from those providing the goods and services we all consume. Manufacturing, retailers, agriculture, medical, and all sorts of government services, including our military, use fossil fuels directly or electricity generated from fossil fuels. Because our emissions include only those that occur within our borders, the emissions from goods we import are not included. As I have previously stated, studies have shown that United States consumption-based emissions are as much as 35% more than our in-border emissions [7].

Most households and businesses can control how they power their vehicles and the structures they own. Controlling emissions beyond this requires that we influence those supplying us either through our buying choices, or the policies the government we elected put in place. Achieving zero fossil-fuel emissions by 2050 means taking personal action and having like-minded neighbors, suppliers, and governance. You cannot do it alone, but you can influence others through your actions!

Challenges and Advantages

Powering our world using renewable energy introduces many changes in how we use and store energy. Although we have the technology to make the transition a reality well before 2050, some of it is unfamiliar to many and not yet available at scale. The transition is also being opposed by the most powerful industry on Earth. The fossil-fuel industry's organized efforts to disseminate disinformation and to create fear about using renewable energy, along with our normal human tendency to resist change, have caused many people to hesitate or even openly appose renewable energy. Let us look at some of the most common concerns people have.

Electric Vehicle Cost

Are electric vehicles too expensive? Although there are plenty of examples of expensive luxury electric vehicles, most electric vehicles now cost close to internal combustion powered vehicles of comparable features, interior space, and function. And after factoring in available credits, rebates, and significant savings on energy and maintenance over their lifetime, their total cost of ownership is lower than comparable internal combustion vehicles. As electric vehicle production volumes grow, the manufacturing cost will continue to fall well below that of internal combustion vehicles. This is because they are so much easier to build compared to the thousands of parts that make up the power and driveline systems of internal combustion vehicles. As battery prices continue to drop, electric vehicles will become even more affordable.

Electric Vehicle Energy Cost

The cost of energy for internal combustion and electric vehicles depends on where you live and how you source your electricity. As I am writing this, the average price-per-gallon of regular gasoline in New York is $3.731, in Texas it is $3.264, and in California it is $5.341. The average electric utility price per kWh in New York is $.22, in Texas it is $.14, and in California it is $.29. This means the cost of driving the average 25-mile-per-gallon light vehicle in New York is $.149 per mile, in Texas it is $.13 per mile, and in California it is $.214 per mile. The average cost of driving an EV that can travel 4 miles per kWh in New York is $.055 per mile, in Texas it is $.035 per mile, and in California it is $.073 per mile. Driving on battery electric power costs between one-third and one-fourth of driving on gasoline power. Over the typical 150,000-mile life of average gasoline powered light vehicles in the United States, the energy savings driving the EV would be $14,100 in New York, $14,250 in Texas, and $21,150 in California (See Electric Vehicle Energy Cost Exhibit). And if you have home solar to power your electric vehicle at less than $.09 per kWh, the EV cost-per-mile is less than $.023. Powering electric vehicles costs a lot less than powering vehicles with fossil fuels.

Electric Vehicle Maintenance and Reliability

Electric vehicles have few moving components to wear out and little that need regular service–washer fluid, tire rotation, wiper blades, etc. Electric vehicle friction brake parts last longer because much of the slowing of the vehicle is accomplished by generating electricity through regenerative braking. Tires on electric vehicles tend to wear more quickly due to the added weight of the battery pack.

The first-generation Nissan Leaf suffered from short battery life. This has been the source of many "scary" stories about premature battery failure. Unlike today's electric vehicles, they did not have effective battery cooling systems or charging management software. Battery packs do lose capacity over time and with the number of charging cycles. Tesla reported in 2021 that their Model S and Model X batteries retain about 90% of their original capacity at 200,000 miles [42]. Most electric vehicle battery packs will outlive the vehicle. It is also true that because electric vehicle motors and drive systems are so durable, it often makes sense to replace the battery pack when battery performance falls off if the vehicle is otherwise in good condition. This is why there are many million-mile EVs out on the roads.

A fleet study of United States government-operated fully electric vehicles reports 40% lower maintenance costs compared to internal combustion vehicles [43]. According to AAA, the average cost for vehicle maintenance in 2023 was $.0983 per mile. Saving 40% over the average 150,000-mile vehicle life amounts to almost $6,000. Not spending as much time at and going to and from dealers, fuel stations, or repair shops adds even more to the savings.

Electric Vehicle Charging

Connected Charging

Never having to visit gasoline stations is a major convenience advantage of electric vehicles. Overall convenience depends partly on how available vehicle charging is. When I am asked how long it takes me to charge my electric vehicle, I often say "Less than 15 seconds" because that is how long it takes to connect to my garage charger. Taking hours to charge is irrelevant because it will be parked there anyway.

Renters often do not have access to chargers where they live. New multi-unit residential building codes often require electric-vehicle-ready wiring in parking areas. Rental property owners are recognizing the advantages of offering vehicle charging. Several companies offer charger programs for rental properties that restrict access and manage the billing to authorized residents. And, if there are assigned parking spaces, it usually is not very expensive to simply install a lockable outlet wired to the appropriate meter. People who drive between 20 and 30 miles per day, with an electric vehicle range of 250 miles or more, will often charge their vehicle only once a week to ten days.

Three levels of battery charging are available for electric vehicles. Level 1 uses standard household 120-volt electrical outlets, typically drawing 12 amps, producing 1.44 kW (W = voltage × amps), and supplying about .1 miles per minute for typical electric vehicles. Level 2 uses a standard 240-volt electrical circuit, like those used for electric clothes dryers and electric ranges, typically drawing 40 amps, producing 9.6 kW, and supplying about .64 miles per minute for the same electric vehicles. This is more than 6 times faster than the level 1 charger example. Level 2 chargers come in amperage ratings of from 15 to 80 amps. The speed of charging varies directly with the amperage. My level 2 garage charger draws 20 amps and is plugged into a 25-amp circuit previously used for an electric clothes dryer. Both level 1 and level 2 chargers supply alternating current to a rectifier built into the vehicle that converts it to direct current to charge the battery pack. Public level 2 chargers are found at work, hotels, parking areas, and other locations where vehicles are typically parked for an extended period. Most electric vehicles come with a portable charger that can be plugged into standard household 120-volt or 240-volt outlets. Many electric vehicle manufacturers and dealers also offer low-cost level 2 charger installation.

Level 3 chargers supply direct current (DC) electricity to the vehicle battery pack and come in a variety of charging levels ranging from 50 kW to 350 kW. These "DC Fast Chargers" are found along commuter traffic corridors, many travel destinations, and at shopping areas. Electric vehicle fast charging speed is influenced by battery temperature and state of charge. A cold battery will charge more slowly, as will one that is nearly discharged. As the cold battery warms, charging speeds up. Charging speed slows again as full capacity nears. Electric vehicles can accept different levels of DC fast charging ranging from 50 kW to more than 300 kW. When connected to a level 3 DC fast charger, the lower of the ratings between the car and charger will apply. For example, a 2023 Chevrolet Bolt that can accept up to 50 kW charging will be charged at that rate when connected to any fast charger delivering 50 kW or higher. A Tesla Model 3 that can accept up to 170 kW will be charged up to that rate when connected to a fast charger delivering at 170 kW or higher. With the Tesla Model 3's range per kWh of 3.95 miles, this equates to 11.2 miles per minute. A fast charge at this rate will deliver 200 miles of range in less time than it takes to stretch your legs and buy a beverage, about 20 minutes.

For most people, who drive under 40 miles per day and have access to a charger where they park for long periods, level 1 or level 2 charging is all they will need for routine local driving. Fast charging makes road trips convenient and solves the charging problem for those who do not have a charger where they routinely park, serving much like retail fuel stations do for internal combustion vehicle drivers. In-car navigation systems and smart phone apps do a good job of assisting drivers to find available chargers and to plan recharging on road trips. There are already many convenient fast charging stations along our highways and in high traffic areas. The companies providing them are ramping up the number of installations as electric vehicle sales continue to grow at a rapid pace. In the end, when we have transitioned to all-electric driving, we will likely have about as many fast charger stations as we now have retail gasoline stations.

Induction Charging

Another form of electric vehicle charging that is emerging uses wireless charging similar to smart phones. This utilizes induction coils imbedded in the roadway to charge the vehicle when it passes over. The vehicle must have a compatible receiver that passes sufficiently close to the induction coil. Although placing this technology throughout all our roadways is prohibitively expensive, there are some applications where it makes a lot of sense. One is where there are fixed routes run repeatedly throughout the day, such as in transit systems. Having induction chargers spaced throughout the route allows for electric busses to operate with a smaller battery pack and to not require lengthy stops for charging. The Kansas City International Airport bus system transitioned to induction charged buses in 2023. Major cities, like Seattle, Washington, are deploying this technology for their transit buses.

Electric Vehicle Battery Safety

Few things instill a sense of fear more than the thought of driving a vehicle that suddenly bursts into flames. There have been some fires in electric vehicles and the news media has been quick to leverage the "drama" of these incidents. Insurance industry statistics, based on fires per mile driven, tell us that electric vehicle battery fires are extremely rare and much less likely than are gasoline powered vehicle fires.

The potential amount of heat released from an electric vehicle battery is much less than that from the fuel of an internal combustion vehicle. Should a fully charged all electric Ford Mach-E with a range of 308 miles have a battery pack fully discharge, it would release about 90 kWhs of energy. Should the fuel of a conventional 25 mile per gallon gasoline powered vehicle with enough gasoline to travel the same 308 miles catch fire, it would release 415 kWhs of energy, more than 4.5 times the heat energy released from the Mach-E battery pack. The chances of having a catastrophic vehicle fire are much lower in an electric vehicle.

Electric Vehicles in Cold Weather

The highest market share of electric vehicles in the world is in Nordic countries, with Norway leading the way at more than 50% of registered vehicles and 82% of new car sales in 2023. Electric vehicles work well in cold weather when there is sufficient charging infrastructure. All types of vehicles suffer some loss of performance when operating in cold weather. Gasoline vehicles have a harder time starting, emit more harmful pollution, and use more gasoline in cold weather. Electric vehicle batteries lose some range when the battery pack is cold and they also do not charge as fast. Preconditioning (i.e., warming) the battery pack helps with both. Heating the interior also takes more energy in cold weather. Planning for the time and energy to preheat the vehicle, to compensate for lower range, and for slower charging, are important considerations for driving electric vehicles in cold weather.

Electric Vehicle Convenience

Electric vehicles offer more conveniences than internal combustion vehicles. They do not need to be warmed up before driving – just turn on and go. Their heating, air conditioning and defrosting systems respond quickly. Most electric vehicles offer remote preconditioning to defrost/warm or cool the interior (and battery pack). And because there are no emissions, it can be done even in a closed garage. Electric vehicles have enough battery power to operate the air conditioning or heating for long periods when parked, while producing little noise, or heat, and no emissions. Never going to a gasoline retailer, and seldom going to the dealer or repair shops are big conveniences, and there are no harmful fuel fumes or oil drips to stain the garage or driveway. The electric vehicle driving experience is superior: low noise, excellent control, and powerful acceleration. One common complaint is that because electric vehicles are often equipped with the latest new features and touch screen controls, learning to operate everything can be frustrating at first. Although Tesla has taken touch screen controls to an extreme, this is not so much an electric vehicle issues as it is an issue with new vehicles generally.

Battery Production and Recycling

Lithium battery materials mining has been the subject of considerable environmental and public health concern. Although lithium is a common element, it does not exist in concentrated form in many places. There are two types of lithium mining. Salt flat mining involves the use of water to pump underground salt brine into ponds where the lithium concentrates as the water evaporates. The other method is hard rock mining where lithium-rich minerals are dug up, crushed, heated, and chemically processed to separate the lithium. Both methods scar the surface and, if allowed to, can release harmful chemicals into the surrounding environment. It is up to the governments where these facilities operate to put environmental controls in place. The United States has significant lithium reserves.

Many lithium-ion batteries also contain nickel, zinc, and a small amount of cobalt. Nickel and zinc are abundant metals commonly used in a wide variety of products. Much of the world's cobalt production comes from central Africa. The sharp rise in cobalt price has encouraged artisanal mining there where children are often employed and conditions are unsafe. Cobalt also comes from many other locations, typically as a byproduct of copper and nickel ores. Although the United States has substantial cobalt deposits, our mining is not yet adequately developed to extract it. Many electric vehicles, such as the standard range Tesla Models 3 and Y, and standard range Ford Mach-E, and most stationary energy storage applications use lithium iron phosphate batteries that contain no cobalt. The metals used in lithium-ion batteries are profitably recoverable through recycling.

Heat Pump Cost and Reliability

Air-sourced heat pump heating systems do cost more than conventional gas-fired heating systems. Ground-sourced heat pump systems used in colder climates cost even more because of the inground piping required. When replacing a gas-fired unit, heat pumps will typically also require some additional electrical circuitry. And if the building needs an electric service or main electrical panel upgrade, that adds to the cost. There are many credits and rebates offered that can bring down these upfront costs. The payoff is over the long term as they use much less energy. The savings depend on the price difference between natural gas and electricity and the efficiency difference between the gas and heat pump systems. If the electricity is supplied from rooftop solar, the payback is much sooner. The expected life of heat pump systems is similar to traditional gas and electric systems.

Transportation

Globally, all forms of transportation accounts for about 15% of greenhouse gas emissions [44]. Developed nations have a much higher share. As the developing world expands its use of fossil-fuel powered transportation, which is the course most developing countries are now on, global emissions from transportation will rise significantly. This is one of the areas fossil-fuel suppliers are promoting as they work to keep their oil and profits flowing. As zero emission transportation evolves, it must find a home in the developing world to keep the petroleum dependency from becoming entrenched there.

On-Road Transportation

On-road transportation accounts for about 30% of United States greenhouse gas emissions [45]. In states such as California, with a mild climate and long commutes, it is near 40%, not including upstream emissions from producing the fuels [46]. For many Americans this is the single largest source of their direct greenhouse gas and other pollution emissions. Each gallon of gasoline burned releases 20 pounds of carbon dioxide into the atmosphere. Adding upstream emissions from the extraction, refining, distribution, and marketing of gasoline increases the total to 25 pounds per gallon [47]. For the average light vehicle in the United States that travels 15,000 miles per year at 25 miles per gallon, that equals one pound of carbon dioxide per mile and 15,000 pounds of carbon dioxide per year. Because diesel fuel contains a higher proportion of carbon, it releases about two pounds more carbon dioxide per gallon than gasoline when burned.

On-road fossil fueled transportation is responsible for much of the air pollution that is so harmful to our health. Operating electric vehicles releases zero direct emissions, though if powered by fossil-fuel generated electricity, some upstream emissions must be considered. In West Virginia, where nearly all the electricity is generated from coal, each kWh of electricity produced releases about 2 pounds of carbon dioxide [48] and plenty of other pollution. With an EV achieving about 4 miles per kWh, that puts carbon dioxide per mile at one-half pound when powered by West Virginia generated electricity. As to the average for United States generated electricity producing .85 pounds of carbon dioxide per kWh, the above EV will release just .2125 pounds of carbon dioxide per mile. As electricity generation transitions to renewable sources, carbon dioxide and the other pollution emissions from producing electricity will drop to zero. Those who have renewably generated electricity to charge their vehicles are already there.

Electric versions of nearly every type of vehicle are already on our roads. We have electric motorcycles, passenger vehicles, SUVs and pickup trucks, commercial light trucks, heavy-duty delivery and box trucks, class eight "big rig" tractors, fire trucks, waste collection trucks, dirt haulers, and busses. They all offer significant energy and maintenance cost savings over internal combustion powered vehicles, and with zero pollution! As production scales up and electric vehicle prices continue falling, the choices available will expand to cover all of our desires.

Electrification of the trucking industry is of special importance because diesel powered trucking is responsible for about one-quarter of on-road transportation's greenhouse gas and smog producing oxides of nitrogen, and a major portion of transportation black carbon particulate pollution. Battery electric powered trucking will significantly lower energy and maintenance costs. The savings during the typical 750,000-to-1,000,000-mile life of one of these vehicles will be in the hundreds of thousands of dollars. Electrification will transform the trucking industry over the next decade.

How about hybrids? These vehicles utilize both internal combustion and electric power to propel the vehicle. An electric generator is used to assist the friction brakes when slowing and stopping the vehicle. The energy recovered by the generator is stored in a battery and is later used to assist propelling the vehicle. The high efficiency of electric power makes a significant improvement in gas mileage. Many hybrids use lightweight materials, have aerodynamic low-profile designs, and utilize power transmission systems that help the internal combustion engine operate within a range where they are most efficient. The combined effects can yield ratings of over 50 miles per gallon. The same technology when applied to larger profile and heavier vehicles also improves fuel mileage, though not as dramatically. Plugin hybrid vehicles operate the same but have larger batteries and electric motors to support 25 to 40 miles or more of all electric driving. The gasoline engine comes on when extra power or interior heat is needed, and when the battery is nearly empty as the vehicle reverts to hybrid mode. If charged regularly they have the advantage of zero carbon operation for typical daily commute distances while offering a range with gasoline power comparable to conventional internal combustion vehicles.

Many automotive manufacturers, and some automotive industry reviewers, have publicized hybrids and their plugin versions as being a better choice than fully electric vehicles for environmentally minded buyers. A hybrid achieving 50 miles per gallon will release half as much carbon dioxide as a 25 mile per gallon vehicle. This is an improvement, but still .5 pounds of carbon dioxide is released for every gasoline-powered mile, and all the other harmful emissions that any internal combustion vehicle produces are still produced. We will not solve the climate or air quality crises by putting more carbon dioxide and pollution into the atmosphere. Driving hybrids or plugin hybrids instead of fully electric vehicles will make things worse.

When Tesla demonstrated that there was a big market for electric vehicles and experienced soaring stock valuations, the other auto manufacturers were caught off-guard. Most now find themselves in the uncomfortable position of not having significant electric vehicle production capacity, along with well-developed supply lines to produce EVs profitably. To appeal to the market looking for low carbon transportation, they had no choice but to push their existing hybrid technology to buy time to develop the engineering, supply chain, production lines, and other expertise required to produce and sell fully electric vehicles profitably.

There is also an internal combustion bias that has influenced the automotive industry. Most auto manufacturers have automotive engineers in senior leadership who cut their teeth on internal combustion power. They identify with fossil-fueled vehicles. Electric vehicles are outside their realm of experience, expertise, or preference. This caused many companies to hang on favoring what they knew as they remained doubtful that battery power would take off. They were asleep at the switch.

There is also bias among new car dealers, the automotive service industry, and internal combustion engine (ICE) vehicle enthusiasts who fear their businesses, professions, and lifestyles will be threatened by electric vehicles. Collectively all this fear, along with disinformation seeded by fossil fuel interests, has created a good deal of resistance and misinformation aimed at derailing the transition to electric vehicles. Many of these same people, along with their fossil-fuel industry enablers, have no apparent concern about the contribution to climate change or air pollution from burning fossil fuels.

To calculate your annual carbon dioxide emissions from on-road transportation, simply calculate how many gallons of gasoline or diesel you use in a year and multiple by the carbon dioxide released by each gallon when burned. For example, if driving a gasoline powered passenger car that achieves an above average 35 miles per gallon and driving 20,000 miles per year, the annual carbon dioxide emissions will equal 14,275 pounds of carbon dioxide per year.

Rail Transportation

Much of the world's rail systems are already electrified. In the United States, most of the freight rail lines rely on diesel-electric power. These locomotives are powered by an electric motor using electricity generated by a diesel engine. They could be powered by electricity from a battery train car or cars equipped with a combination of chemical batteries and hydrogen fuel cells. If chemical battery equipped, they could also recover kinetic energy by incorporating regenerative braking when traveling downhill and stopping. Electricity could also be supplied through sources along the route, either overhead wires, an energized third rail, or through induction charging placed between the rails. With 160,000 miles of rail line in the United States, there is great potential to harvest solar and wind energy along the rail right-of-way. All of these electrification options will significantly lower energy costs and eliminate rail diesel emissions.

Water Transportation

Water transportation is a significant contributor to global greenhouse gas and air pollution emissions. Diesel-powered ferries are especially harmful polluters and responsible for about as much global warming emissions as aviation. There are already many ferries in service powered by batteries. With their lower operating cost and zero emissions, we can expect that electrified ferries will become the norm as the fossil fueled units are retired. Some ferries powered by hydrogen fuel cells are now in service. Time will tell if the cost of green hydrogen can come down enough to make them competitive with battery electric power.

Oil burning cargo and container ships are the dirtiest of all water transportation vessels. The fuel they use releases large amounts of black carbon soot, sulfur dioxide, and other pollution. Globally they release about as much carbon dioxide as aviation. Shipping companies are testing several approaches to address their emissions. Alternative fuels include biofuels, and green hydrogen. Adding high tech sail power assist and solar panel power is also being tested. Some battery powered cargo vessels are already in use for shorter routes. Cruise ships face the same challenges as cargo ships. Battery power is a good fit for many smaller commercial and pleasure craft applications.

Air Transportation

Aviation is responsible for about 3% of global greenhouse gas emissions. On average, traveling by commercial airline releases about one-half pound of carbon dioxide per passenger air mile [49]. This means that for most people traveling alone, it is often a better climate choice (and safety choice) to fly commercial than driving the average 25 mile per gallon gasoline powered vehicle, which releases one lb. of carbon dioxide per mile. Private aircraft and short route aviation emissions per passenger mile are of course much higher.

Chemical battery powered aircraft are already being applied to short distance routes. Replacing the kerosene-based jet fuel used in turboprop and jet aircraft will be difficult. Biofuel kerosene has been produced, but scaling its production to replace fossil kerosene has yet to be demonstrated as a practical approach. Synthetic kerosene made from green hydrogen and carbon is a possible replacement, though it too poses a lot of challenges. All the kerosene type fuels have the advantage of being compatible with existing jet and turboprop technology. Using hydrogen directly as a combustion fuel will require entirely different aircraft because of the large space required for fuel storage, as well as different engines. Aviation may prove to be the most difficult form of transport to decarbonize.

Heating and Cooking

Space and Water Heating

Burning fuels for space and water heating is a significant source of air pollution and greenhouse gas emissions. To compare the carbon dioxide produced from burning the various fossil fuels, I will use what is commonly called a *"Therm"* as the standard measure of heat. The heat content of a therm is 100,000 British Thermal Units (BTU) and is equal to 29.3 kWhs of energy. A typical cold climate household using natural gas for space and water heating will use between 4 and 6 therms per day in the winter. This varies considerably based on home size, how well it is insulated, and many other factors including how efficient the heating unit is. Our central California coast home averaged 1 therm of natural gas per day annually for cooking, water heating, and space heating prior to transitioning to all electric. Standard efficiency gas-fired heating appliances are typically between 80% and 90% efficient, meaning 10% to 20% of the heat produced from combustion goes up the chimney. The newest high efficiency gas furnaces and water heaters are rated as high as 95%. This rating is known as the *coefficient of performance* and is calculated by dividing the energy supplied for heating the space or water, by the energy used. Electric resistance heating, which is also common for water and space heating, has a 100% coefficient of performance.

In a renewable powered world, space and water heating will be primarily provided through electric heat pumps. The most common heat pumps we all have experience with are refrigerators, freezers, and air conditioners. Heat pumps do not use energy to generate heat, but instead use energy to harvest heat that already exists. They accomplish this by pumping a liquid refrigerant into a low-pressure heat exchanger, known as an evaporator, where the refrigerant transitions to a gas as it absorbs heat from the surrounding environment. The hot gas is then pumped into a heat exchanger, known as a condenser, where the absorbed heat is released into the surrounding environment as the gas transitions back to a liquid. The liquid is then returned into the evaporator where the process repeats.

Heat pump furnaces and water heaters deliver a coefficient of performance of from 300% to over 400%, meaning they provide three to four times more heat energy than the energy used to operate the unit. And if powered by renewably generated electricity, they will be responsible for producing no carbon dioxide or other pollution. Even if powered by the dirtiest coal generated electricity, the electricity used will still produce less carbon dioxide and other pollution than will their fossil fueled heating alternatives.

Although few homes or other structures use coal today for heating, those that do, release about 21 pounds of carbon dioxide for every therm of heat produced. Wood is also used, either in fireplaces or stoves for space heating. Although wood is a renewable fuel, it is one of the most polluting and harmful fuels available. Even "clean burning" wood pellet stoves produce very harmful levels of fine particulates inside and out of the structure. Heating oil is commonly used in some parts of the United States. It produces about 16.3 pounds of carbon dioxide per therm. Natural gas produces 11.6 pounds of carbon dioxide per therm, while propane produces 13.9 pounds. All of these combustion fuels also produce a lot of other harmful pollution [50].

To illustrate how much energy can be saved using a heat pump, I will compare an 85% efficient forced air gas furnace with an Energy Star rated heat pump furnace that averages 350% efficiency. The heat energy in a therm translates to 29.3 kWhs of energy. If 15% of the energy produced from burning the gas is lost up the chimney, that means only 24.9 kWhs of energy is contained in the heat delivered into the space being heated. To produce that much heat energy using a 350% efficient heat pump will require only 7.1 kWhs of electricity, less than one-fourth the energy!

Several types of heat pumps are available for space heating. It is common to replace a forced air furnace with a heat pump that uses the existing duct system and includes a heat/cold air handler assembly to replace the furnace with an air source heat pump compressor located outside. Ductless systems utilize a separate interior heat/cold exchanger and exterior heat pump for each room or zone. These are sometimes selected even when replacing a forced air unit because they are the most efficient, with no heat loss through leaks in the duct system. Water heating systems use heat pump water boilers to replace the fossil fuel boiler. Tankless electric resistance water heaters work well in many instances, but are only 100% efficient and require a lot of electricity capacity to heat the water quickly.

There are other significant advantages to heat pumps over burning fossil fuels. Ductless units offer more precise control because each room or zone has a separate thermostat. Air handlers used in ducted systems use variable speed motors that start and run quietly and keep the space evenly heated without much noticeable cycling. Many people also tend to take advantage of the heat pump efficiency savings by keeping the space a little warmer during cold weather and cooler during heat spells. The safety advantages of heat pumps over burning fuels are significant. Without a flame and no highly combustible fuel there is little risk of carbon monoxide poisoning, fire, or explosion.

Electric Ovens and Cooktops

Most residential and commercial cooktops and ovens today are powered by either natural gas or electric resistance coils. When natural gas is used, significant emissions of harmful hydrocarbons like benzene, and other pollution such as nitrogen dioxide and fine particulates, are released directly into the room. Even electric resistance cooktops produce considerable pollution as dust, cooking drips, and spatter settles on the hot surface and burns. Most residential and many commercial kitchens are not well ventilated, causing these spaces to be dangerous to the health of all present. Both natural gas and electric resistance cook tops create a lot of heat with as much as one-half being released into the room. These cooktops are also the source of fires as flames or glowing hot surfaces encounter combustible materials.

Electric induction cooking uses a magnetic coil below the glass cooktop surface to excite the molecules in the pan placed on the surface to heat the pan. This has the advantage of using much less energy because there is little waste heat going into the room. The risk of fire is also greatly reduced. There is no pollution introduced into the space beyond what may come directly from what is in the pan. The heating of the pan is also more even than either natural gas or electric resistance cook tops. Induction cooktops have a big advantage when a lot of heat is desired quickly. The speed boil feature cuts the time to boil water by about one-half.

Induction cooking requires pans with bottoms that a magnet will stick to. This includes all cast iron, steel, and other pans designed for induction cooking. If a pan is removed and not replaced after a short time, the cooktop will sense it, sound a tone, and turn off. No more burners left on after removing the pan! Because all the heat is in the pan, the glass cooktop surface never gets very hot, so spills and spatter are not cooked on–just wash and wipe dry.

One sign of the superiority of electric induction cooking is the number of professional chefs and culinary schools that are embracing it. The equipment does cost more than conventional electric and gas cooktops, but the use of much less energy, healthier air, easier cleanup, and much lower kitchen heat makes the transition well worth it.

Proper Ventilation

The worst air pollution most people encounter is in their home. Cooktops, ovens, and wood-burning fireplaces and stoves, are common sources of harmful indoor air pollution. Microwave cooking also introduces harmful pollution from the food being cooked. Most microwaves today are not vented to the outdoors. Many above-cooktop microwaves, which do feature a vent fan merely vent the fumes away from the microwave and into the room. Being aware of our exposure to harmful pollution generated from cooking will bring us to face the need to effectively ventilate all cooking areas.

Inexpensive air quality monitors are now available to alert us to unhealthy levels of carbon dioxide, carbon monoxide, ozone, fine particulates (PM2.5), nitrogen dioxide, and volatile organic compounds. Once you have a good tool to detect such pollution, it will not take you long to curb your indoor wood burning, your use of natural gas, and smoke producing open-pan roasting, braising, and frying. It will also open your eyes to the exposure we all face from outdoor pollution entering our homes. Having a PM2.5 monitor inside our homes will also alert us to the need to have adequate particulate filtration.

Appliances

Appliance manufacturers are constantly adding efficiency improvement to their products. Because most small appliances do not use much electricity, these improvements are not typically enough to motivate people to replace appliances before they wear out. But several categories do warrant consideration for early retirement. Heat-pump clothes dryers use about one-half the energy of gas or electric resistance units. The money saved can offset the early cost of replacement. Unlike conventional dryers, heat-pump dryers do not need to be vented, making them a little more versatile. They come in 120-volt and 240-volt designs. They also come in combination configurations where the washer and dryer use the same drum–just put in the clothes, set how you want to wash and dry, and it all happens automatically. Drying time is considerably longer in the 120-volt units.

Lighting is another area where early replacement of older inefficient devices makes sense. Compared to traditional incandescent and florescent bulbs, light emitting diode (LED) lighting uses as little as 10% of the electricity and lasts up to 25 times longer. Although this technology is now common, we still a have a way to go to completely replace our less efficient florescent and incandescent lighting.

Equipment, Tools, and Machines

We have long used tools powered through wired electricity for construction and home tasks–everything from drilling, vacuuming, and sawing. With the availability of powerful battery power, we are now seeing electric power replacing fossil fueled powered tools. Small gasoline engine powered equipment, like leaf blowers, trimmers, and lawn mowers, have been the target of some important government policies that are accelerating the transition to electric power. Air pollution from small gasoline engines is excessive and hazardous to anyone nearby. Because of this, and the loud noise they produce, many communities have been banning their use. In 2021, California sent a powerful signal to the manufacturers of these machines indicating that their sale would be banned starting in 2024. That law is now in force and the new battery-powered machines the manufacturers have produced are proving to be more than capable of doing the job. Although they may never recognize it, many thousands of landscaping laborers and homeowners will live healthier and longer lives as a result.

As with on-road transportation, battery-powered machines are now available to replace fossil fueled farm tractors, excavators, forklifts, and all the other machines used in construction and agriculture. Portable energy storage is also available to handle recharging when there is no grid connection. There are even some battery-powered mining haulers that carry heavy loads downhill as they are recharged entirely by regenerative braking, which supplies enough energy to climb back up the hill empty for the next load.

Industry and Manufacturing

Existing electrified industrial and manufacturing activities will transition to renewable energy as the grid and local electric generation does. Eliminating carbon dioxide emissions from the most intense direct uses of fossil fuels to produce especially high heat, such as iron and steel production, will require entirely new facilities and significant investments. Globally and here in the United States, iron and steel production still largely rely on coal. There are effective zero carbon dioxide emission alternatives available. A process called *green hydrogen iron reduction* produces pure iron from iron ore (i.e., iron oxide) without the use of coal or releasing any carbon dioxide emissions. Green steel is produced using an electric arc blast furnace.

Electric induction furnaces are already commonly used in foundry applications to melt metals such as iron, steel, copper, and aluminum. Electric resistance furnaces are in common use for heat-treating of metals and pottery work. Electronic heating with radio and microwave equipment is widely used in industry for heating wood, plastics, and ceramics. Electric annealing ovens and furnaces are used in glass manufacturing. Electron-beam furnaces are used for production and refining of high-purity metals such as titanium, vanadium, and exotic alloys. The technology is also used in electron beam devices for cutting, welding, and machining metals. Large-scale heat pumps are also in use in many industrial applications.

Concrete Production

Concrete production is responsible for about 8% of global carbon dioxide emissions, nearly three times that of aviation. Extracting and hauling the materials used to make and deliver concrete can all be electrified. The largest carbon dioxide emission source in this industry is cement manufacturing. This is the material that binds the rock and sand in concrete. Calcium oxide (CaO) is the essential ingredient in cement. It is produced from crushed calcium carbonate rock, such as limestone, that is heated to high temperatures causing the calcium carbonate ($CaCO_3$) molecular bond to be broken, freeing the carbon and calcium to combine with oxygen to produce carbon dioxide and calcium oxide. The use of fossil fuels for this heating also releases a lot of carbon dioxide. Although electric cement kilns have been in use for many years, they are not common because they cost more. The newest electric cement kiln designs have the added advantage of yielding a concentrated stream of carbon dioxide that can be easily captured to prevent it from escaping into the atmosphere. This is a good example of how we could use government policy to level the cost among cement providers and force change to eliminate this excessive source of emissions.

8 - FOSSIL FUELED POLITICS

High levels of economic inequality lead to imbalances in political power, as those at the top use their economic weight to shape our politics in ways that give them more economic power. – Joseph Stiglitz, Nobel Laureate economist, and public policy analyst

Wealth and Political Power

We have the know-how and the resources to replace fossil fuels throughout our economy. Do we have the political will to do so?

Fossil-fuel suppliers throughout the world are working hard to continue profiting from our use of their fuels. Their enormous wealth is used to influence our politicians, and in some countries, they are the government. Although domestic oil companies are influential in the United States, we are not as dependent on fossil-fuel revenues as nations such as Russia, Saudi Arabia, Iran, and Iraq. Ours is a diverse, highly developed, and resilient economy. Though we are one of the world's largest oil and gas suppliers, like most of the developed nations of the world, we are dependent on fossil-fuel suppliers from around the world. For example, the majority of California's crude oil comes from outside of California, mostly from Ecuador, Columbia, Saudi Arabia, and Iraq. As international oil suppliers manipulate oil supply to keep global prices up, all of us in the United States feel the tug of BIG OIL on our pocket books.

The United States can absorb the disruptions from switching to renewable energy. We will lose fossil-fuel related jobs, companies will go out of business, and some will lose investments as we stop using fossil fuels. Our booming renewable energy industry will continue to grow, offsetting these disruptions, driving our continued economic health, and reinforcing our energy independence. But for fossil-fuel companies, their investors, and those nations dependent on fossil-fuel export revenues, this will not be a welcome change. We can expect they will try to do anything they can, and I mean ANYTHING, to prevent the renewable energy transition from succeeding.

We have already seen countries like Saudi Arabia and Russia meddling in world politics to support fossil-fuel friendly politicians and policies in other countries. And the global fossil-fuel funded lobbies and propaganda machines are more active than ever. As pressure increases from ordinary citizens around the world to take climate saving action, fossil-fuel interests are blocking efforts to implement climate action, spreading disinformation, and weakening the notion of objective truth and faith in science. They are also encouraging political polarization and the breakdown of bipartisan cooperation, undermining democracy, and trust in government, promoting autocratic movements, diluting individual rights, and making governments more responsive to special interests than to their citizenry. Sound familiar? We are experiencing this all across the developed and developing world. A relatively small number of the wealthiest few are in a struggle with all the rest of us to maintain their extravagant lifestyles and political power at our expense.

Fossil Fuel Industry

Back to the Cave

During a forum at the November, 2023, United Nations Climate Conference (COP28), Sultan Al Jaber, Chief Executive of the United Arab Emirates' state oil company ADNOC said, "There is no science out there, or no scenario out there, that says that the phase-out of fossil fuel is what's going to achieve 1.5C.," referring to holding global warming to 2.7^0 Fahrenheit (1.5^0C) over preindustrial times. He further elaborated that a complete phase-out of fossil fuels would "take the world back into caves."

Although the Sultan's denial or ignorance of the science was disturbing, his continuing sentiment about returning to cave living tells us a great deal about the underlying fear of his nation and other **fossil fuel revenue-dependent nations**. Their primary source of wealth is from the extraction and export of fossil fuels. Without this good fortune, the Sultan's nation would not be far removed from a relatively meager existence. To the energy consuming nations of the world, the transition to renewable energy represents a more prosperous future. But to wealthy **fossil fuel revenue-dependent nation** leaders, the loss of their export windfall threatens their way of life. Of course, many of these nations also face serious threats from climate change, but that is seen as the lesser problem to their authoritarian leaders.

Some wealthy **fossil fuel revenue-dependent nations** are diversifying their economies and investment portfolios, and taking other steps to reduce their dependence on fossil-fuel exports. Because many of them have high potential for renewable energy generation, there is some hope of exporting renewable electricity, or through production of green hydrogen-related fuels. But the windfall of wealth they enjoy today from simply exporting fossil fuels will not be replaced. To avoid economic collapse and political destabilization as the world transitions to renewable energy, the major nations of the world may need to provide aid and loan packages to some fossil-fuel exporting nations, while increasing education, and technical and other support, all with the aim to establish economies that can thrive on their own once global fossil-fuel use ends. In the end it will not be the **fossil fuel revenue-dependent nations** or fossil-fuel companies who put an end to fossil fuels. That will only happen when we consumers no longer demand to use fossil fuels. We are in charge!

Fossil-Fuel Suppliers

Countless entities are involved in exploring, extracting, transporting, refining, distributing, and retailing fossil fuels. The largest private, investor-owned, and nation-owned companies are the most visible and powerful of those actively funding efforts to block renewable energy development. Calling them out for this is justified. But to villainize all the people this industry employs does not help solve the climate crisis problem. These are businesses that are responding to our collective demand for their products. The supply of fossil fuels is not the problem. It is our demand that drives the supply.

As in other types of businesses, fossil-fuel companies hire people to maximize the value of their company and to do so within the laws and regulations where they operate. If they are allowed to operate in ways that harm people or damage the environment, it is both their moral failure and a failure of government. Like any well-run business, they have an eye on demand for their products over time and another on profitably supplying what the market demands. When we see companies like Exxon-Mobil and Chevron investing in new oil and gas reserves, it is because they see demand for these products continuing into the future.

This industry knows how damaging their products are. It is when they use their wealth and influence to prevent the transition to renewable energy that they step over and into the truly evil side of the moral line. The political dilemma is that we need sufficient fossil fuels today for economic and political stability. As renewable energy is increasingly deployed, demand for fossil fuels will drop and fossil-fuel companies will recognize that much of their fuel reserves have no value. The bottom line is that our demand for fossil fuels is what is perpetuating its use. Until we cut off the demand, emissions will continue.

Renewable Production

Many fossil-fuel companies have investigated transitioning to renewable energy production. None have found a path to do so in a significant way. Little of the know-how, infrastructure and other resources used in supplying fossil fuels are useful in a world powered by renewable energy. The business models are completely different. If people could easily produce gasoline at home and at low cost, the oil companies would not have a business. The same is true of natural gas and coal. Anyone who has renewably generated electricity to power their vehicles, homes, and businesses has little need for expensive polluting fossil fuels.

There are a few areas where fossil-fuel companies do have technical expertise that may be applied to a renewable energy-powered world. They have long produced hydrogen from fossil fuels and have experience storing and handling it. Having used carbon dioxide injection to increase oil and gas field production, they also have experience handling carbon dioxide. And in recent years, some have invested in carbon dioxide capture technology. By combining these skills, it may be possible to produce hydrogen from methane while capturing and storing underground the carbon dioxide released from the methane steam reforming process plus any carbon dioxide released from the fossil fuels used to power the process. The problem with this is that it does not measure up financially or practically when compared to simply producing hydrogen using renewable electricity from water.

An extension of their carbon capture technology would be to apply it to open-air situations to literally suck carbon dioxide out of thin air. With a present carbon dioxide atmospheric concentration of 420 parts per million (i.e., .042%), this is much more difficult than extracting carbon dioxide from environments where there are more concentrated streams of it. Fossil-fuel companies have touted direct air capture technology as a means for drawing down our carbon dioxide while allowing us to continue burning fossil fuels. Of course, this would not do anything to reduce all the other harmful fossil-fuel pollution. Is this just another delaying tactic to cause people to hold off switching to renewable energy? Until there are working plants that can demonstrate that this works, is affordable, and that there are either places to store the carbon dioxide or other uses of it that will keep it out of the atmosphere, this will remain a wishful distraction. The EPA estimates the operational cost of direct air capture will be as much as $630 per metric ton (i.e., 2,205 pounds) of recovered carbon dioxide. That translates into an additional cost for gasoline of $7.15 per gallon. Renewable energy is already much lower cost before piling on more cost to cover direct air carbon dioxide capture. The money will be better spent converting to renewable energy.

Feeling the Heat

Fossil-fuel companies and their employees are feeling the literal heat of global warming as well as the figurative heat from their continuing promotion of fossil fuels. People working in fossil-fuel companies are not living in a bubble where they are protected from the reality of the world around them. Many are conflicted about working in an industry responsible for supplying products that release such harmful emissions. How do they justify their continued work?

Fossil fuels have transformed our civilization by powering astonishing improvements in productivity, comfort, and convenience. The fossil-fuel industry is justifiably proud of these accomplishments. Fossil-fuel companies and their employees feel an obligation to supply the energy the market demands. And according to the oil and gas companies, demand shows little sign of abating anytime soon. Jobs at the major oil and gas companies tend to be stable, pay well, and have excellent benefits. Justification is not hard when you are valued, well rewarded, secure, and feel a sense of purpose.

But this armor of justification has some kinks. It is now well known that as far back as the 1960s, fossil-fuel companies clearly understood that the use of their products would cause the climate to warm. They withheld this information from the public. Later when outside scientist recognized the same, they denied it or downplayed the impact it would have. They lied.

Fossil-fuel companies have increasingly used misleading claims to make their products and activities appear to be more environmentally friendly than they are. This greenwashing does not change the underlying reality that the continued use of fossil fuels will be devastating to our economic prosperity, public health, and the natural world. More lying.

Fossil-fuel companies continue to actively campaign to block renewable energy adoption through "investments" in political influence, trade organizations, think tanks, public relations firms, hired pseudoscientists, and consultants. It frequently takes the form of misleading information that is cleverly not expressed in the name of fossil-fuel companies. The disinformation includes anything that will cause people to fear the use of renewably powered electrification to replace fossil fuels. For example, falsely claiming that electric vehicles are more fire prone, that they do not work in cold or hot weather, that the battery packs will not last long, or that you cannot use them on road trips are good examples of this sort of activity. The list of disinformation topics and distraction tricks is seemingly endless. The collective effect is to prevent us from focusing our efforts on reducing our use of fossil fuels and to create the impression that renewables are not up to the task. All of this is to protect the demand for fossil fuels, even as climate destabilization from our warming climate is causing devastating harm across the globe. Their deceit continues.

Backlash

The fossil-fuel industry's long record of deception has already undermined their credibility with the public, politicians, investors, and even their employees and potential recruits. These days, most recent high school graduates are fully aware of the reality of global warming and the devastating consequences their generation is facing if we continue using fossil fuels. This is presenting some challenges for recruiting and retaining critical skills. Renewable energy companies are finding success recruiting in cities like Houston, Texas, where there is a lot of science and engineering talent looking to make a better world.

Is there liability or illegality in deception? Although some legal actions have been taken against fossil fuel companies, little has come of it. Investor-owned fossil-fuel companies are increasingly feeling the heat from their shareholders. Some of this is in the form of disinvestment by people who no longer want to be involved in funding fossil fuels because of the industries' efforts to delay the renewable energy transition. Others are selling their shares because they believe the companies are overstating future demand and future earnings. This is not so easy for many ordinary investors who find their retirement and investment funds include shares of fossil-fuel companies. Although many of the major funds have eliminated "Sin Stocks" such as tobacco, gambling, and weapons manufacturers, fossil-fuel suppliers remain in most portfolios.

Fossil-fuel companies are experiencing some pressure from activist investors who use their considerable holdings to influence company leadership to change how they direct the company. Some have attempted to direct fossil-fuel companies to shift toward renewable energy production. The fossil-fuel companies fight these efforts because they do not want to hasten the transition to renewables, nor to do anything that will reduce future demand for their fuels. Maximizing shareholder value depends on having strong demand for fossil fuels well into the future, regardless of the harm it may cause.

Living in the Sewer

We are treating our thin slice of atmosphere as an open sewer. In 2022 humans dump more than the 346 billion pounds of carbon dioxide equivalent (CO2e) into the atmosphere every day [51]! Our daily share here in the United States was over 38 billion pounds–112 pounds per person [52]. In addition to this, our use of fossil fuels adds enormous amounts of many harmful forms of pollution into the atmosphere. In a renewable energy powered world, all of these harmful emissions will come to an end!

Treating our atmosphere as a dumping ground is very costly. Economic modeling reveals that our global economy today would be at least $20 trillion larger without the global warming we have already experienced (2). The World Bank estimates global annual health cost from air pollution at $8.1 trillion [53]. Without these costs our global economy would be nearly 30% larger! On our present course with fossil fuel emissions continuing to climb, the drain on our economy will grow ever larger.

We are eroding our wealth and moving backward economically, only to enrich fossil-fuel suppliers. A renewable energy-powered world will have no fossil-fuel emissions. And because our energy costs will be lower, transitioning to renewable energy will remove the economic burden of fossil fuel use and increase our wealth and standard of living.

Detailed research from Stanford University's Atmosphere/Energy Program of 145 nations indicates that the global transition to renewable energy is achievable within 13 years at a total cost of $62 trillion [54]. This is a bargain price to eliminate the ever-growing economic cost from fossil-fuel air pollution and greenhouse gas emissions. Transitioning to renewable energy AS SOON AS POSSIBLE is the common-sense thing to do!

9 - MAKING IT HAPPEN

Our greatest responsibility is to be good ancestors. – Jonas Salk, virologist, and medical researcher

The greatest threat to our planet is the belief that someone else will save it. – Robert Swan, explorer, and environmental activist

Polls show that most people in the United States believe climate change is real and a serious concern. Having reached this final chapter, you have been exposed to what we must collectively do to stop both the warming of our climate and the air pollution from our use of fossil fuels. You have probably taken some action, or at least have ideas of how you should act to address your personal contributions to these problems. Realizing that you cannot do it alone, you may be feeling challenged to understand how to influence others to help achieve real action across our country and beyond.

Profoundly Obvious

It is easier to sell things that people want.

When I first heard this sentiment during a marketing lecture, it first struck me as absurdly obvious. As the lecture continued, I found that it encapsulated a profoundly important thesis. Understanding what people want is central to influencing their behavior. This is especially relevant to the transition to renewable energy. Solving the climate crises is about eliminating demand for fossil fuels by motivating people to want to transition to renewable energy. This is the marketing imperative of the renewable energy transition.

While protesting new pipelines, fracking, and all sorts of fossil fuel exploration and production activities may draw a lot of attention, build community, and bring satisfaction to climate activists, these activities do very little to directly reduce demand for fossil fuels. The global market has significant capacity to supply what the market demands. When projects are blocked or exploration delayed, supply disruptions will soon be filled by other suppliers. But cut demand and fossil fuel use will stop, regardless of how abundant the supply.

All of the many modern conveniences we now take for granted have come to us through a period of transition where we came to adopt the new and cast off the old. Lower cost is already moving many businesses and individuals to make the switch to renewable energy. Although there are many tangible factors like lower cost and convenience that people respond to, it is the intangible that is frequently a more potent force of change. The threshold that will trigger change is often when a person does not like how they are representing themselves to the world. There is an old automotive industry marketing saying: "What you drive is who you want to be." You see this in automotive advertising where it is all about lifestyle and image. Many of our buying choices, especially those that are visible to others, have a significant aspirational component.

We now have the ability to more affordably and conveniently power all of our needs using renewable energy. And the many ways our use of fossil fuels harms all of us is well known. In a world increasingly aware of these truths, a person who continues using fossil fuels is representing themselves as someone willingly harming all those around them, as well as future generations the world over. The marketing objective of the renewable energy transition is to inspire people to want to represent themselves to the world as someone who is considerate, caring, and informed because they choose to power their lives using renewable energy. The moral slogan of the renewable energy age: Good people do not burn fossil fuels.

The merits of transitioning to renewable energy are profoundly obvious!

Separating Science from Politics

We live in a time when politicians who are backed by fossil-fuel interests tend to express different views about how we should be responding to climate change compared to most everyone else, including many of their constituents. We also live in a time of extreme polarization based on differing views of certain cultural and social norms, what is commonly called *identity politics*. The identity impulse can be so dominate that people end up voting based on who they identify with rather than what is in their best interest overall. It is not uncommon for the polarization to be so strong that one side is against anything the other side favors. This is of course absurd because there are many things we all support, like clean water, bridges that do not fall down, and the local school sports team. When politicians oppose renewable energy, we have an opportunity to change the focus to the common good–things we can all agree on that are more important than the culture war issues. Clean air, lower energy costs, and preventing runaway climate destabilization are goals we can all agree on.

In the past, much of the opposition to renewable energy was attributed to a lack of understanding of climate science. For decades, many pro fossil-fuel politicians called climate change from global warming a hoax. These days, it is not so easy to dismiss it in this way. Not only is it now obvious that climate change is real, many more people who are now voting have been educated about climate science. In addition, this newest generation of voters is anxious about the prospect of an uncertain climate future and resent those who failed to act in the past. The electorate increasingly wants climate action. We have seen this shift recently in the bipartisan passage of the Infrastructure Investment and Jobs Act in 2021 and the Inflation Reduction Act of 2022, which included significant components to support development and use of renewable energy.

It is important to be sure all who represent you in government understand that you expect them to support a rapid transition to renewable energy. You should also understand what their position is and any actions they have taken on the subject one way or the other. Understanding who is funding them is also important. And be sure to share what you learn as you influence others to vote.

Leading by Example

It is a lot easier to influence people to follow by your example. This does not mean you need to wait until you are living a zero-emission lifestyle to begin to influence others to support the transition to renewable energy. Once you have done something and have a plan for everything else, you are leading!

It took us several years to eliminate our emissions from personal transportation and our home. There are plenty of decisions to be made and distractions that can get in the way. Some homes may need electric service upgrades to accommodate additional electric devices. And when you have gas appliances that are working just fine, it can be hard to justify replacing them before their service life is over. An electric vehicle came first for us because transportation was our largest source of emissions, and we needed a new car. We did the easy things first, like replacing our inefficient lighting with LEDs and subscribing to electricity generated from 100% renewable energy, which is not an option everywhere. Then we needed a new clothes washer, so we purchased a heat pump combination clothes washer and dryer. Our rooftop solar installation was bundled with a new roof and a main electrical panel upgrade to provide future circuits for an induction range, and heat pumps for space and water heating. An induction range came next to replace our tired gas range. Over the next year we explored the available heat pump space heating and water heater options. Finding contractors in our area with experience installing and servicing this technology was not easy at the time. Once this was resolved, we went ahead replacing our gas furnace and gas tankless water heater. The final step was to remove the gas meter and top it off with an electric fireplace log! Generating the added electricity for the heat pumps required yet more solar panels. By then the solar contractor had a long backlog, so it was another six months before the additional panels were working.

Although we continue to be exposed to pollution released from the many sources around us, we have eliminated our household and personal transportation pollution and greenhouse gas emissions while reducing our annual energy cost by over $3,000 (See Annual Energy Cost Savings Exhibit). With inflation, our annual savings will no doubt increase because our solar cost per kWh is locked in for 20 years. Our renewable powered life is safer, more comfortable, more convenient, and costs a lot less. Not only are we now able to be an example, the knowledge we gained in the process has helped us inform others.

Talking to People

Achieving cooperation and taking collective action requires a good deal of consensus. Often our differences get in the way of even opening a dialog. So how do we move forward down the road to renewable energy when there are so many potholes of distraction, disinformation, and disagreement?

Talking About Global Warming and Climate Change

Most people avoid talking about global warming and climate change. Many are afraid of confrontation, ridicule, or simply feel they lack the knowledge. Although learning about the causes and consequences of global warming, and about renewable energy helps build confidence to engage in conversation, the polarization around the subject can be intimidating. As the changes in our climate are increasingly more obvious, most people are willing to concede that our climate is changing and humans are causing it. The conversation is shifting to discover what we can and should do about it.

Finding Common Ground

Achieving broad consensus to transition to renewable energy requires shared common goals. We are all in this together and we must all come together regardless of our other differences. Casting a wide net means being inclusive and tolerant. To engage in discussion with others, it is essential to discover what common ground you share with them. Finding things that you both care about or that most people in a group care about is usually easy.

One way of diffusing disagreement over the causes or consequences of global warming is to change the conversation to focus instead on the benefits of transitioning to renewable energy. This often works well because it appeals to our personal wellbeing and financial motives. We all face the reality of the cost of living, the challenges of achieving financial security and the spectacle of global wealth inequality. Our use of fossil fuels rather than renewable energy harms our health, costs more, and is driving global wealth inequality. This is fertile common ground for most people.

We live in a time when fossil fuel revenue-dependent nations and their industry partners have a stranglehold on the global economy. As their products are traded on international markets, they collude to restrict supply to keep prices and profits high. Some, such as Russia and Iran, use their fossil fuel wealth against the United States and our allies. And at times they manipulate supply to apply political pressure, as Russia has against European countries, or to influence political outcomes in other countries. Transitioning to renewable energy will put an end to this kind of foreign influence and profiteering. You will find plenty of common ground to be considered here.

Because the global economy now depends on fossil fuels, we also live in a time when the United States has been forced to protect the international fossil-fuel supply lines that we, and our allies depend on. We have fought wars and suffered great loss of treasure, blood, and lives to protect Middle East oil supplies. This is one of the most significant subsidies we provide to the global fossil-fuel industry. We spend our money and sacrifice many lives to protect their fuels and profits. In a renewably powered world, energy independence will be the norm across the globe. This is good common ground for anyone concerned about how we use our military and our high military spending.

The true cost of fossil-fuel energy is obscured by many hidden economic, health, and environmental costs. In addition to the major military subsidy just described, fossil-fuel suppliers also receive staggering tax advantages, lax regulation, and bargain access to fossil-fuel resources on public lands. Throughout our country, fossil-fuel companies have exerted their political power to win favorable terms at every level. The bottom line is that we all pay a lot more for fossil fuels than is apparent from our out-of-pocket cost. The International Monetary Fund estimates that 2022 global fossil fuel industry subsidies amounted to $7 trillion, which was equal to about 7% of the global economy [55].

Our use of fossil fuels is the source of an enormous amount of pollution and environmental harm. Fossil-fuel air pollution and the effect it has on our health has already been covered in previous chapters. But all the other types of pollution have not. We all remember the big oil spills, such as Exxon Valdez and BP Deepwater Horizon. We have experienced many lessor spills through the years that have contaminated our streams, rivers, lakes, beaches, and land. And there are countless examples of spills, fires, and explosions in our communities, at refineries, along rail lines and pipelines, and on our roadways that have damaged the environment and harmed so many people. Visiting abandoned coal, gas, and oil extraction sites, you quickly grasp the enormous scope of the damage left behind. The environmental damage at active sites is equally alarming. This is a dirty and extremely hazardous business!

The spectrum of how sensitive people are to causing harm to others is broad. The closer the potential harm is to individuals or their immediate family, the more concerned people tend to be. And for some, the thought of knowingly causing harm to others, even those they will never personally encounter, is repulsive. Asking someone what we should do for the people being forced to abandon their homes from sea level rise, drought, or extreme heat, will tell you a little about their perspective. If they do not recognize any responsibility, which is not uncommon, you know something about their concern about others. Asking them about what we should do to protect their family and future descendants from extreme weather caused by our warming climate will reveal more about their sensitivity to potential harm touching those close to them. If they do not care about others, then focus on the harm coming to them or their family.

For many people, protecting the natural world is a strong motivator. This does not mean they have connected the dots between how our fossil-fueled global economy is threatening the outdoors they so love or how they could help prevent it. If you establish that a person or group has an interest in the natural world, you have an opportunity to begin making those connections.

Security has many levels. Having a secure home from the threat of wildfire and extreme weather is a growing concern. Food, water, and economic insecurity are heightened by climate change. The threat of political instability from climate-driven refugees is another. The Defense Department has named climate destabilization a major threat to our national security [56]. These are all possible areas of common ground.

Let Us Discuss

You can start conversations about taking action to transition to renewable energy in many ways. Start with those close to you. Family, friends, neighbors, coworkers, and members of your social, service, and religious groups are all good candidates. Starting conversations with strangers can be a little harder. There is often something about the person that creates an opening to talk. I have started many conversions with Toyota Prius drivers by saying how much I liked my Prius and now love my battery electric vehicle even more. They invariably ask why. And if you notice where someone may be from or a favorite sports team, such as a sticker on their car, or perhaps signage on a garment, you can pose a friendly question that may be an opening to talk. The persona you project can also stimulate conversation. I often wear a button or clothing that identifies me as being interested in addressing climate change. This does help start conversations. People frequently say, "I like your button." It often leads to more, such as what I am doing to reduce my emissions, etc. Driving an electric vehicle produces a lot of questions that often continue in more depth. And my yard sign describing how our all-electric house that produces more energy than it uses while saving us money and eliminating our emissions has led to a lot of discussions, and some new friends (See YARD SIGN Exhibit).

Studies have shown that only about 1 in 20 individuals are not open to discussing or making changes to address climate change. If you encounter someone who appears to be one, do not fret. If they are truly dismissive, providing facts will not likely change their attitude. If you have someone willing to engage in conversation, start by being a good listener and by being kind. You may have to ask some questions to help you gain an understanding of what the person believes or has concerns about. Be positive. People fear loss and naturally assume that change means the loss of something. When someone expresses a fear of loss, it is okay to acknowledge it if it is real, but respond in a balanced way with the positives. Be respectful and counter false information with facts or simply by acknowledging that the science says differently. Kindly disagree without being disagreeable. If they ask about what the science has to say, or even better, say something that just is not so, you now have an opening to talk more.

The range of knowledge about climate science among the public is of course wide. It is easy to get lost in the weeds. Keep it simple. Use plainspoken language. Wherever the conversation goes, I try to end with a few important points.

- Our use of fossil fuels is releasing massive quantities of greenhouse gases and other pollution into the atmosphere that is causing our planet to warm, threatening our lives, and damaging our natural world–the world that supports all life.
- Clean renewable energy technology is readily available and completely capable of affordably and conveniently replacing fossil-fuel energy.
- A renewable energy powered world will be healthier, more prosperous, and far safer.

Get Serious

As I have discussed transitioning to renewable energy with a lot of people over the years, I have heard plenty of excuses to continue with business as usual. At the root of all of the excuses is a failure to take the climate crisis seriously. As the Swedish environmental activist Greta Thunberg has said regarding how we should all be reacting to the climate crisis: "I want you to panic. I want you to feel the fear I feel every day.;" "I want you to act as if the house is on fire, because it is." When your house is on fire, one does not come up with excuses to ignore it, let alone add more heat to stoke the fire! The only way to prevent the harm we are all exposed to from fossil fuel pollution and climate change is to stop using fossil fuels.

Should a person feel guilty when they burn fossil fuels? Well, yes, they should. Knowingly contributing to the human suffering and environmental destruction fossil fuels are causing should make one feel guilty. An informed and caring person should be open to transitioning to renewable energy that is clean, convenient, and cost less. They may not yet know how to change, but they should be open to it.

There are excuses that relate more to having other priorities. Most people have busy lives and continuing with business as usual is the easy way out. Addressing the climate crisis deserves to be top of mind. Nothing else will matter if your climate becomes unlivable. Many people have taken a step or two to reduce some of their fossil fuel emissions, only to stall, as if they have done their part. They are not serious about solving the climate crisis. Going through a greenhouse gas emission audit is a great way to help a person reinvigorate their good intentions and set new priorities.

It can be hard to get passed the "I cannot afford it" excuse. This is usually a cover for not really knowing what the cost and savings would be. Asking if they have actual quotes of the work and expected savings is a good way to uncover if a person is serious about avoiding the impending climate catastrophe. It is also important to ask why it is okay for them to continue to put the cost of their emissions on all the rest of us while they wait to act.

The "Get Serious" test should also extend to the government policies we are supporting. If someone is not voting for leaders who support the renewable energy transition, they are not serious about solving the climate crisis.

Ask for Action

Taking action to eliminate global warming emissions and to encourage the transition to renewable energy can be a challenge for many people. Most have no idea what the emissions are from their various sources or where to begin the analysis. A good place to begin is with the emissions that individuals can personally control, such as from personal transportation and at home. It takes some effort to gather the information such as, miles driven and average miles per gallon, therms of natural gas used, kWhs of electricity used and their utilities' carbon dioxide emission per kWh. Many people will have a hard time coming up with the information and doing the math. To prevent them from giving up, another approach is to focus on the likely largest source of emissions or the ones that are easiest to transition to renewable energy. If the person drives a lot, that may be the place to begin. If they have an old gas fired furnace, water heater, cooktop, or clothes dryer, these may be good candidates for replacement with more efficient electric options. Other efficiency improvements, like improved insulation and LED lighting, are often easy changes to implement. And if their utility offers a zero-carbon electricity choice, that is an easy first step. Going through an analysis of your own emissions will prepare you for guiding others.

For most of us, the majority of our share of emissions is upstream from our personal lives where we have little direct control. Although it is not always easy to influence the organizations that provide us with the goods and services we consume, you can make your desires known. First, search out those organizations that are taking action to reduce their emissions and send your business their way. If a company is doing something about reducing their emissions, they will likely be publicizing it. Letting the companies you buy from know that you want to support the transition to zero emission renewable energy will help motivate them. Avoiding goods that are shipped from afar is another step to reduce emissions.

Local, state, and federal agencies can be influenced simply by making your priorities known. Mayors, councilors, supervisors, and elected representatives at every level need to hear from all of us. And of course, how we vote is important.

I have been observing the world's reaction to the climate crisis for many years now. It has often felt as if most people were doing nothing at all. Global emissions have continued to climb while the fossil-fuel industry expands their plans to supply even more. The potential harm from climate change has been well publicized for decades and we are now increasingly experiencing the effects. It has been like a slow-motion disaster unfolding in front of our eyes with most people waiting for everyone else to do something about it. Despite these past disappointments, we now have good reasons to be optimistic about preventing catastrophic climate destabilization. We have choices. Make it your choice.

"Our descendants will look back on these past few decades in wonder. Regardless of what action we take now, they will likely find our past denial of human-caused global warming and our inaction to adequately address it as unforgivable. What is uncertain is just how much they will suffer. If we fail to act soon, they will most certainly suffer far more or perhaps fail to exist at all." – James Leach, *The Sustainable Way*

Although this is the end of this book, make it your beginning to be a good ancestor by committing to support the rapid transition to renewable energy.

EXHIBITS

2050 U.S. Land Area for Solar

- Annual solar electricity production required = 5 trillion kWhs
- Square mile area of lower 48 States = 3.12 million sq miles
- Feet per mile = 5,280 ft
- Annual average production per solar panel = 500 kWhs
- Average solar panel size = 17.6 sq ft

Calculations:

- Electricity production required per sq mile: 5 trillion kWhs / 3.12 million sq miles = 1,602,564 kWhs per sq mile
- Electricity produced per sq ft of solar panel: 500kWhs / 17.6 sq ft = 28.4 kWhs per sq ft of solar
- Square ft of solar needed per square mile: 1,602,564 kWhs per sq mile / 28.4 kWhs per sq ft = 56,428 sq ft solar per sq mile
- Square feet per square mile: 5,280 ft × 5,280 ft = 27,878,400 sq ft per sq mile
- Percentage of square mile required for solar panels: 56,428 sq ft solar panel per sq mile / 27,878,400 sq ft per sq mile = .2%

Electric Vehicle Energy Cost

Gas Vehicle @ 25 MPG vs. Electric Vehicle @ 133 MPGe

	New York	Texas	California
Gasoline / Gal	$3.731	$3.264	$5.341
Utility electricity / kWh	$.22	$.14	$.29
Gasoline cost / mile	$.149	$.13	$.214
Utility electric cost / mile	$.055	$.035	$.073
Utility electric saving / mile	$.094	$.095	$.141
150K mile savings	$14,100	$14,250	$21,150
Solar electricity / kWh	$.09	$.09	$.09
Solar electric cost / mile	$.0228	$.0228	$.0228
Solar electric savings / mile	$.1262	$.1072	$.1912
150K mile savings	$18,930	$16,080	$28,680

Annual Household Energy Savings

- Average mpg of the gasoline powered vehicles before switching to all electric vehicles = 35 mpg
- Household electricity used before electric vehicles and transition to electric heat pump clothes drying, heat pump space and water heating, and induction cooking = 9 kWhs per day
- Average natural gas used before transitioning to all electric appliances = 1 Therm per day.
- 2023 Average price of residential natural gas (CA) based on actual 2022 average cost per therm = $2.20 per therm
- 2023 Average price of regular gasoline (Pacific Grove, CA) = $5
- 2023 miles driven = 15,000 miles
- 2023 Electricity used per day (including EV charging) = 28 kWhs
- 2023 Utility bundled price electricity (CA, PG&E) = $.38 / kWh
- Electricity cost based on 10,220 kWh annual production and 25 year depreciated of $21,000 initial investment (NEM 2.0) ($21,000/25/10,200 kWh) = $.08 per kWh

Annual energy cost without electrified household

- Gasoline: 15,000 miles / 35 mpg × $5 = $2,143
- Natural Gas: 1 therms per day × 365 days × $2.20 = $803
- Electricity: 9 kWhs / day × 365 days × $.38 / kWh = $1,248
- Total Energy Cost: = $4,194

Annual energy cost of EVs, solar, and electrified household

- Electricity: Utility connection fees $288
- Electricity: 28 kWhs per day × 365 days × $.08 = $818
- Total Energy Cost: = $1,106

Annual estimated savings: = $3,088
California Net Metering 2.0: The credit value of a kWh supplied to the grid is equal to the price of pulling a kWh off the grid

Extra Atmospheric Carbon Dioxide

Each part per million of carbon dioxide in the atmosphere represents 7.82 gigatonnes of carbon dioxide (Oak Ridge National Laboratory).

140 ppm x 7.82 x 10^9 tonnes = 1.095 x 10^{12} tonnes of CO_2.

2205 lbs. per metric ton (tonne)

1.095 x 10^{12} x 2205 lbs. = 2.414475 x 10^{15} lbs.

Yard Sign

☀ This Old Electric House

This all-electric 100-year-old home produces more electricity than it uses. We have significantly lowered our energy cost and eliminated the hazards and harmful emissions from using natural gas. The temperature inside is always comfortable, we have plenty of hot water, love induction cooking, and we and our neighbors are breathing cleaner air.

Watch the video: https://youtu.be/Z8scY_d-dps

SUGGESTED READING

No Miracles Needed: How Today's Technology Can Save Our Climate and Clean Our Air, Mark Z. Jacobson, Professor of Civil and Environmental Engineering and Director of Atmosphere/Energy Program at Stanford University, 2023 Cambridge University Press

Saving Us: A Climate Scientist's Case for Hope and Healing in a Divided World, Katharine Hayhoe, Atmospheric Scientist, Professor of Political Science, and Director of Climate Science Center at Texas Tech University, Chief Scientist for the Nature Conservancy, 2022 Atria/One Signal Publishers

The New Climate War: The Fight to Take Back Our Planet, Michael E. Mann, Presidential Distinguished Professor, Department of Earth and Environmental Science at University of Pennsylvania, 2022 PublicAffairs

Our Fragile Moment: How Lessons from the Earth's Past Can Help Us Survive the Climate Crisis, Michael E. Mann, Presidential Distinguished Professor, Department of Earth and Environmental Science at University of Pennsylvania, 2022 Hachette Book Group

Regeneration: Ending the Climate Crisis in One Generation, Paul Hawken, Environmentalist, Entrepreneur, and Bestselling Author, 2021 Penguin Books

REFERENCES

1. **Jacobson, Mark Z.** *No Miracles Needed.* s.l. : Cambridge University Press, 2023.

2. **Bilal, Adrien and Känzig, Diego R.** *THE MACROECONOMIC IMPACT OF CLIMATE CHANGE.* Economics, Stanford University; Northwestern University. Cambridge, MA : NATIONAL BUREAU OF ECONOMIC RESEARCH, 2024.

3. *Who has contributed most to global CO2 emissions?* **Ritchie, Hannah.** 2019, Our World in Data.

4. **statista.** *Per Capita CO2 2022.* [Online] https://www.statista.com/statistics/270508/co2-emissions-per-capita-by-country/.

5. *U.S. and China on Climate: How the World's Two Largest Polluters Stack Up.* **Friedman, Lisa.** July 19, 2023, New York Times.

6. **Mengpin Ge, Johannes Friedrich, Leandro Vigna.** 4 Charts Explain Greenhouse Gas Emissions by Countries and Sectors. *World Resource Institute.* [Online] [Cited: June 28, 2024.] https://www.wri.org/insights/4-charts-explain-greenhouse-gas-emissions-countries-and-sectors.

7. **David Burch, Principle Environmental Planner.** *Bay Area Consumption-Based Greenhouse Gas Emissions Inventory.* s.l. : Bay Area Air Quality Management District, 2016.

8. **worldmeter.** *GDP by Country.* [Online] https://www.worldometers.info/gdp/gdp-by-country/#:~:text=GDP%20by%20Country%20%2D%20Worldometer, $17%2C963%2C200%2C000%2C000.

9. Climate Change: Global Temperature. [Online] [Cited: July 1, 2024.] https://www.climate.gov/news-features/understanding-climate/climate-change-global-temperature#:~:text=The%20roughly%202%2Ddegree%20Fahrenheit,significant%20increase%20in%20accumulated%20heat..

10. **Ziska, Lewis H.** *Rising Carbon Dioxide and Global Nutrition:.* [Online] https://www.ncbi.nlm.nih.gov/pmc/articles/PMC9003137/.

11. **Norberg, Goyer, Clarkson.** Impact of effects of acid precipitation on toxicity of metals. *NIH National Library of Medicine.* [Online] https://pubmed.ncbi.nlm.nih.gov/3908087/.

12. *Atmospheric CO2 levels can cause cognitive impairment.* **Karnauskas, Kris.** April 21, 2020, Life Science News.

13. *Indoor CO2 concentrations and cognitive function: A critical review.* **Du B, Tandoc MC, Mack ML, Siegel JA.** s.l. : National Institute of Health, November 2020, PubMed.

14. *Our ability to complete complex, strategic tasks could drop 50% by 2100, scientists warn.* McFall-Johnsen, Morgan. December 2019, Business Insider.

15. *Ambient carbon dioxide concentration correlates with SARS-CoV-2 aerostability and infection risk.* Haddrell, Allen. April 2024, Nature Communications.

16. *Climate and Infectious Diseases.* s.l. : CDC, March 21, 2024, National Center for Emerging and Zoonotic Infectious Diseases.

17. Particle Pollution and Your Patients' Health. *EPA.* [Online] https://www.epa.gov/pmcourse/patient-exposure-and-air-quality-index.

18. Air Quality Guidelines. *World Health Organization.* [Online] https://www.c40knowledgehub.org/s/article/WHO-Air-Quality-Guidelines?language=en_US#:~:text=The%20WHO%20guidelines%20state%20that,3%20%2D%204%20days%20per%20year..

19. Fitzpatrick, Beheraj, Rose Dickey. Air pollution has improved in the San Francisco Bay Area since 2012. *AXIOS San Francisco.* [Online] April 28, 2023. https://www.axios.com/local/san-francisco/2023/04/28/air-pollution-quality-san-francisco-bay-area.

20. American Lung Association. *Estimated Prevalence and Incidence of Lung Disease.* [Online] September 2024. https://www.lung.org/research/trends-in-lung-disease/prevalence-incidence-lung-disease/methodology#:~:text=About%2015.6%20million%20adults%20(6.4,diagnosed%20with%20chronic%20lung%20disease..

21. Air Pollution. *World Health Organization.* [Online] https://www.who.int/health-topics/air-pollution#tab=tab_1.

22. NASA Explore. *How Atmospheric Water Vapor Amplifies Earth's Greenhouse Effect.* [Online] https://science.nasa.gov/earth/climate-change/steamy-relationships-how-atmospheric-water-vapor-amplifies-earths-greenhouse-effect/.

23. Scripps. SCRIPPS RESEARCHERS ASSESS THE FUTURE OF CLIMATE IN CALIFORNIA. *Scripps Institiution of Oceanogrophy.* [Online] https://scripps.ucsd.edu/news/scripps-researchers-assess-future-climate-california.

24. NOAA Climate. *Climate Change: Global Sea Level.* [Online] https://www.climate.gov/news-features/understanding-climate/climate-change-global-sea-level.

25. Goldman-Sachs. Electric car battery prices are going back down faster than expected. *electrek.* [Online] https://electrek.co/2023/11/20/electric-car-battery-prices-are-going-back-down-faster/.

26. NOAA. Annual Greenhouse Gas Index. [Online] 2023. https://gml.noaa.gov/aggi/aggi.html.

27. IEA. CO2 Emissions in 2022. *IEA 50.* [Online] https://www.iea.org/reports/co2-emissions-in-2022.

28. AGU. BLACK CARBON IS MUCH LARGER CAUSE OF CLIMATE CHANGE THAN PREVIOUSLY ASSESSED. *Advanced Earth and Space Sciences.* [Online] Jan 15, 2013. https://news.agu.org/press-release/black-carbon-is-much-larger-cause-of-climate-change-than-previously-assessed/.

29. NASA. Aerosols and Their Importance. *NASA Earth Sciences.* [Online] [Cited: June 27, 2024.] https://earth.gsfc.nasa.gov/climate/data/deep-blue/aerosols.

30. Tree Facts. *Arbor Day Foundation.* [Online] [Cited: JUly 20, 2024.] https://www.arborday.org/trees/treefacts/.

31. CO2 Absorbed. *ONETREEPLANTED.* [Online] [Cited: July 20, 2024.] https://onetreeplanted.org/blogs/stories/how-much-co2-does-tree-absorb?_pos=1&_sid=fc05d7eda&_ss=r.

32. Newton, James D. *Uncommon Friends: Life with Thomas Edison, Henry Ford, Harvey Firestone, Alexis Carrel, & Charles Lindburg.* s.l. : Harcourt Brace Jovanovich, 1987.

33. Davis, UC. What is Solar Power? [Online] https://www.ucdavis.edu/climate/definitions/how-is-solar-power-generated.

34. eia. What is U.S. electricity generation by energy source? *U.S. Energy Information Administration.* [Online] https://www.eia.gov/tools/faqs/faq.php?id=427&t=3.

35. EIA. Annual Energy Outlook 2023. *U.S, Energy Information Administration.* [Online] https://www.eia.gov/outlooks/aeo/electricity_generation/.

36. *Cost controversies still inflame critics of Plant Vogtle expansion as kilowatts go online.* Dunlap, Stanley. June 5, 2023, Georgia Recorder.

37. Association, American Public Power. How Much Water Our Electricity Uses. [Online] [Cited: August 14, 2025.] https://www.publicpower.org/periodical/article/how-much-water-our-electricity-uses.

38. Administration, U.S. Energy Information. Use of energy explained. [Online] [Cited: August 14, 2025.] https://www.eia.gov/energyexplained/use-of-energy/electricity-use-in-homes.php.

39. Webber, Michael E. *Thirst for Power.* s.l. : Yale University Press, 2016.

40. Battery Technology. *Form Energy.* [Online]
https://formenergy.com/technology/battery-technology/.

41. *WPTO Studies Find Big Opportunities to Expand Pumped Storage Hydropower.* ENERGY.GOV. june 13, 2022, Office of Energy Efficiency & Renewable Energy.

42. INSIDEEVs. Tesla: Battery Capacity Retention Averages 90% After 200,000 Miles. [Online] https://insideevs.com/news/525820/tesla-battery-capacity-retention-90/.

43. *Battery-Electric Vehicles Have Lower Scheduled Maintenance Costs than Other Light-Duty Vehicles.* US Department of Energy. 2021.

44. Greenhouse Gas Emissions. *Global Greenhouse Gas Overview.* [Online] [Cited: July 7, 2024.]
https://www.epa.gov/ghgemissions/global-greenhouse-gas-overview.

45. Transportation, Air Pollution, and Climate Change. *Carbon Pollution from Transportation.* [Online] [Cited: July 1, 2024.]
https://www.epa.gov/transportation-air-pollution-and-climate-change/carbon-pollution-transportation.

46. CARB. California GHG Emission Inventory. [Online]
https://ww2.arb.ca.gov/ghg-inventory-data.

47. Schildgen, Bob. How much CO2 is generated by producing and transporting a gallon of gas? *Sierra Magazine.* [Online]
https://www.sierraclub.org/sierra/ask-mr-green/hey-mr-green-how-much-co2-generated-producing-and-transporting-gallon-gas#:~:text=Take%20a%20look%20at%20their,to%206.7%20pounds%20per%20gallon..

48. Statista. Power sector carbon intensity in the United States in 2022, by state. [Online]
https://www.statista.com/statistics/1133295/electric-sector-carbon-dioxide-emission-rate-by-state-united-states/.

49. Aviation emissions. *Carbon Independent.org.* [Online]
https://www.carbonindependent.org/22.html#:~:text=CO2%20emissions%20from%20aviation%20fuel,CO2%20per%20passenger%20per%20hour..

50. EIA. Carbon Dioxide Emissions Coefficients. [Online]
https://www.eia.gov/environment/emissions/co2_vol_mass.php.

51. UN. Emission Gap Report 2023. [Online]
https://www.unep.org/interactives/emissions-gap-report/2023/#section_0.

52. EPA. Sources of Greenhouse Gas Emissions. [Online]
https://www.epa.gov/ghgemissions/sources-greenhouse-gas-emissions.

53. World-Bank. What You Need to Know About Climate Change and Air Pollution. [Online] https://www.worldbank.org/en/news/feature/2022/09/01/what-you-need-to-know-about-climate-change-and-air-pollution.

54. *Low-cost solutions to global warming, air pollution, and energy insecurity for 145 countries.* Jacobson. s.l. : Royal Society of Chemistry, 2022, Energy & Environmental Science.

55. Fossil Fuel Subsidies. *IMF.* [Online] https://www.imf.org/en/Topics/climate-change/energy-subsidies#A%20Global%20Picture%20of%20Energy%20Subsidies.

56. Climate Change Threats. *USDOD.* [Online] https://www.defense.gov/News/News-Stories/Article/Article/3510772/hicks-defines-need-to-focus-dod-on-climate-change-threats/#:~:text=Extreme%20heat%2C%20floods%2C%20rising%20sea,readiness%2C%20the%20deputy%20secretary%20said..